THE RESILIENT PASTOR

THE RESILIENT PASTOR

Ten Principles for Developing Pastoral Resilience

Mark A. Searby

Foreword by Lyle W. Dorsett

RESOURCE *Publications* · Eugene, Oregon

THE RESILIENT PASTOR
Ten Principles for Developing Pastoral Resilience

Resource Publications
An Imprint of Wipf and Stock Publishers
199 W. 8th Ave., Suite 3
Eugene, OR 97401

www.wipfandstock.com

ISBN 13: 978-1-4982-2363-8

Manufactured in the U.S.A. 04/29/2015

My thanks to Dr. John Walker, founder and director of Blessing Ranch Ministries in New Port Richey, Florida, for his permission to include his paper "Why Leaders Blow Up" in Appendix Ten.

To Linda, my best friend and source of encouragement, and to our two sons and their wives for the joy they have been and the wisdom they have shared during the leadership journey.

CONTENTS

FOREWORD

The church in the early twenty-first century is experiencing an acceleration of some disturbing trends in pastoral ministry. Between 3,000 and 5,000 pastors quit the ministry every month, and these numbers do not include aged pastors who go into retirement. Some statisticians claim that at least 50 percent of America's pastors leave ministry within five years of beginning their ministry. Eight out of ten clergy say ministry adversely affects their family. Nearly half of all ministers suffer burnout and depression. Nearly half of the nation's clergy confess they have a problem with pornography, and few pastors say they have a safe friend to whom they can confess sin and be held accountable to repent. In short, one reason why Christianity is no longer the fastest growing religion in North America is that far too many pastors are blind guides leading the blind. No wonder many observers say that Christianity in the United States is 3,000 miles wide and a quarter inch deep.

Dr. Mark Searby has spent several decades pastoring churches and training future clergy. Keenly aware of the corrosive condition of pastoral leadership in America, this experienced and gifted pastor and teacher does more than wring his hands over this clergy crisis. Indeed, drawing upon personal experience, careful research, and his gift of listening to ministers, he offers the church a rich gift of his thoughtful reflections. *The Resilient Pastor* is not just another book on leadership methods. Instead, this volume is a clarion call to pastors. Searby challenges pastors to stop worrying over the breadth of their ministry and invest in the depth of their ministry.

Foreword

The Resilient Pastor is a fresh, timely, and hopeful book. Here the reader is called to examine and apply ten principles. I am confident that all pastors who read this splendid book will be transformed and strengthened to survive the struggles and adversity common to all of us in ministry.

Lyle W. Dorsett
Billy Graham Professor of Evangelism
Beeson Divinity School, Samford University
and Senior Pastor, Christ the King Anglican Church

ACKNOWLEDGMENTS

I want to express my grateful appreciation to the following men who have taught me much about pastoring and resilience:

Larry Densmore—his passion for Jesus and his investment in my spiritual growth started me on my journey of leadership

Lynn Laughlin—my coach and friend through many years

Bruce Parmenter—his wisdom and counsel have enriched my life and my ministries

Bill Stark—a model pastor/shepherd who showed me leadership grace

Don Green—a servant leader who has been a true teacher to me

Dick Wamsley—my mentor and guide who modeled resilient leadership

Lyle Dorsett—my colleague who graciously prays for me and keeps me focused

In addition, I owe much to my former students at Lincoln Christian Seminary and my current students at Beeson Divinity School who teach me constantly about the challenges to be faced in order to be A Resilient Pastor.

Finally, I am grateful for my two young pastor friends, Marcus and Ben, who allow me to share in their journey of developing pastoral resilience.

INTRODUCTION

He was a twenty-three year old pastor in his second ministry. Struggling to get by financially on a meager salary with a new baby while also working on his MDiv degree, his idealism was quickly fading. After a very difficult beginning to his new ministry in which he followed a much-loved pastor, two very difficult pastoral situations occurred within the congregation. One involved a messy divorce of a church leader, and the other involved some church members who had experienced personal renewal through involvement in a community Bible study group which did not share the accepted doctrine of the congregation. Tension had developed between the young pastor and two of the congregation's elders. Adding to the complexity of the tension was the young pastor's own insecurities and failure to identify some relational aspects of the conflict which were triggered by some of his own "family of origin" issues. At age twenty-three, even though he was in good physical shape, this young leader was taken to a nearby hospital believing that he was experiencing a heart attack. After a thorough physical exam, it was determined that he was experiencing a spastic esophagus brought on by stress. A short time later, he resigned his ministry with no prospect of a new position. Failure was a regular word in his mind and his vocabulary! I was that young pastor!

Through the counsel and encouragement of some godly mentors, I did not give up on ministry leadership. God provided a new opportunity for ministry serving on staff with an experienced, wise pastor who became another important mentor. In addition, the elders and members of our new congregation were loving, grace-filled Christians who came alongside my wife and me and nourished us and helped us to heal.

I learned that ministry is complex, difficult, and costly! It often includes much heartache and pain. At the same time, I learned that it is a wonderful privilege which provides an opportunity to walk with individuals in the most intimate aspects of discovering God's grace. It is possible to become a tool of transformation in their lives through the power of the Holy Spirit as one serves the people of God and seeks to minister effectively during the leadership journey.

A LEADERSHIP CRISIS

We have a leadership crisis today! The crisis is that too many leaders have built upon a faulty foundation or have focused upon the wrong things. Some emerging leaders bring dysfunctional dynamics from past personal history into their attempts to become developed in their leadership role which sabotages their progress. Others have surrendered to false expectations for pastors or cultural measures of success.

As a teacher and mentor to students preparing for ministry leadership, it is painful to observe how many pastors and other church leaders burn out or fail out within five years of beginning their ministries. It is also distressing to reflect on how many of my former colleagues or former students have failed out or burned out of ministry. The statistics vary, but it is commonly believed that approximately 50 percent of pastors do not last in ministry more than five years. In his classic study of leaders, Robert Clinton discovered that 7 out of 10 Christian leaders do *not* finish well.

After serving as a pastor in the local church for twenty-four years, for the past seventeen years I have been involved in teaching and mentoring at two institutions for higher Christian education: Lincoln Christian University (college and seminary) in Lincoln, Illinois, and Beeson Divinity School at Samford University in Birmingham, Alabama. My burden for pastors and emerging pastoral leaders is heavy and personal.

During my tenure in teaching and mentoring emerging church leaders, I have had the opportunity to observe what brings students to seminary, what keeps them, and what resources and experiences they need. In teaching and equipping seminary students (most of whom were preparing for leadership roles in local churches), it has become apparent that some key issues need to be addressed in leadership development. This has also been reinforced by my work in mentoring leaders who are already working in a ministry setting.

These key issues are addressed in the ten principles of becoming a resilient pastor—a leader who finishes well. While the development of understanding historical, doctrinal, exegetical, and ministerial competency materials is assumed as foundational in ministry leadership development, that is not the focus of this book. The focus of *The Resilient Pastor* is on the character development and spiritual formation of the Christian leader which will carry him or her through the challenges of ministry.

Because ministry is more challenging than ever and pastors are facing more demands, now is the time to embrace these principles for pastoral formation. As I observe current leaders in the church, I see many who are feeling overwhelmed, becoming discouraged, then dropping out of leadership roles, or in some cases, out of the church altogether. It is my desire to be used by God to help make a difference and turn this trend around. The challenges facing emerging leaders necessitates that we equip these leaders—not so much with techniques and methods, but rather with a strong foundation that provides them the insights and wisdom to engage their ministries with personal and biblical health, passion, and perseverance.

FOUR ASSUMPTIONS

There are four basic assumptions with which I operate as I approach this subject of pastoral resilience:

1. Struggle and adversity are normal.
2. Self-understanding is crucial.
3. Growth is possible.
4. Resources are available.

Assumption # 1: Struggle and Adversity Are Normal

Struggle and adversity are central to growth and change in a leader's life. Jesus' own ministry began with a time of struggle and adversity under the direction of the Holy Spirit (Luke 4:1–13). Paul's personal testimony is about God's sufficient grace in times of adversity (2 Cor 12:10), and his challenge to other servant leaders is a reminder that God's power is obvious in our times of weakness (2 Cor 4:7–15).

In our human frailty we often want to avoid all pain or struggle. We are a society in which the first response to pain is often medication. Such a response can mask the real issues involved in the pain or struggle, or it can prevent people from enacting the changes in their lives which are needed to experience long-term growth. Resilient leaders learn to embrace the truth that "suffering produces endurance" (Rom 5:3–7) and that it will result in an effective and fruitful life (2 Pet 1:8).

It is not necessary to seek adversity. Struggle and adversity are a normal part of life and leadership. As they occur, it is critical to view them as opportunities for deeper reflection and change.

Assumption # 2: Self-Understanding Is Crucial

Self-understanding is crucial to becoming a resilient leader. All Christian leaders have been shaped by the collective experiences of their lives. Paul recognized how his own life and ministry had been shaped by his early life experiences (cf. Gal 1:11–17; Phil 3:4–8; 1 Tim 1:12–16) yet resulted in his becoming a witness of God's amazing grace.

Our personal journeys may have included many detours along the way or even begun with significant challenges as a result of our circumstances. These experiences do not disqualify us to serve as leaders in God's kingdom. They do not determine us or negate our potential to contribute to the lives of others. However, the experiences of our journey do shape and influence us in significant ways that are important to understand if we want to be healthy, resilient leaders and effective servants with others.

Reggie McNeal makes a pointed and insightful statement concerning the value of spending time in examining our journey in order to understand ourselves better:

> The most important information you will need as a leader—*self-understanding*. This is a different issue than self-preoccupation. Self-preoccupation shows up in leaders who use others in order to achieve their own ambitions. Self-understanding begins and ends with God. This takes time and reflection.[1]

Assumption # 3: Growth Is Possible

Leaders can lead in the midst of adversity and actually become better leaders as a result of the experiences of adversity. Our goal in becoming resilient pastors is to live and minister with others in ways that lead to vitality, joy, and growth *while* facing the adversities of ministry with a solid faith. Our purpose is not just to survive, but to thrive.

The apostle Paul knew that the path that leads to pastoral resilience is difficult, but that adversity must not stop ministry. Thus, he challenged the young leader, Timothy, to persevere in his work in the midst of opposition (2 Tim 4:1–5).

1. McNeal, *A Work of Heart*, xiv.

There are no shortcuts to leadership maturity. Just consider Moses, David, Peter, Paul, or Timothy! Many of our greatest lessons are learned through failure, not success.

We cannot lead faithfully or finish well accidentally! Both must be approached from a perspective that includes an understanding that our development will be life-long, intentional, Spirit-led, and practiced in community with other believers.

Assumption # 4: Resources Are Available

God provides the necessary resources for the development of resiliency. Becoming a resilient pastor is not accomplished by one's own strength, skills, and wisdom. It is developed through a process of relying upon the work of the Holy Spirit as He molds us into the image of Jesus Christ, the greatest servant leader of all time (2 Cor 4:7–12). The resilient pastor depends upon the assurance that he or she is redeemed through the blood of Christ, transformed by the presence of Christ, and nourished by the Word of Christ.

This work does not take place only in isolation, but also in community with others who are experiencing the same transforming process. It is a journey not traveled alone, but with saints past and present. We learn from the examples of those who have gone before us and we learn from the shared wisdom of current mentors and travelers whom God uses in our shaping process.

INTRODUCING THE CONCEPT OF RESILIENCE

The literature on resilience crosses over into many disciplines. In physics, resiliency refers to a material's ability to return to its original form after being compressed or stretched. It is the elasticity of the material. Research on resilience is being conducted in the fields of education, leadership and management, psychology, social services, and family relationships.

> Research points to resilience as being a process that builds over time. It can be described as an ongoing and

> developing fund of energy and skill that can be used in current struggles or the active process of self-righting. . . . So, *resilience is a process of coping with adversity, change, or opportunity,* in such a way as to identify, fortify, and enrich resilient qualities in a person.[2]

There are many definitions or understandings of the term "resiliency." One that helps provide additional insights into the subject is by Dr. Al Siebert:

> Resilience is the process of successfully adapting to difficult or challenging life experiences. Resilient people overcome adversity, bounce back from setbacks, and can thrive under extreme, ongoing pressure without acting in dysfunctional or harmful ways.[3]

My own simple, functional definition is: *Resiliency is the ability to overcome adversity and maintain effective living and leading while experiencing growth.* For the pastoral leader, it involves faithfulness and fulfillment in ministry leadership in the midst of difficult circumstances. The biblical term for resilience is "perseverance" (the biblical term will be expanded upon later in this chapter).

A Brief History

The concept of resilience was developed in the 1970s and finds its origin in the field of psychology. The foundational research project on resilience was begun in 1955 by Emmy Werner. For over 30 years, Werner and Robert Smith followed the lives of over 500 children. This research caught the attention of others in 1992 when they published *Overcoming the Odds: High Risk Children from Birth to Adulthood.*

The study of resilience primarily fits within the "positive psychology" movement which operates from a strengths model

2. Allain-Chapman, *Resilient Pastors*, 18.
3. Siebert, *The Five Levels of Resiliency*, para. 2.

instead of a deficit model. However, the literature on resiliency is definitely multidisciplinary.

> A substantial number of strength-oriented studies followed on the heels of Werner and Smith's work, and today researchers continue to add empirical evidence supporting the premise that resilience is not a fixed-trait phenomenon. Resilience is developmental, it can be learned, and it can be taught.[4]

The insights of Justine Allain-Chapman underscore this point that resilience is developmental. She also describes some important principles which can be learned from Victor Frankl's classic work, *Man's Search for Meaning.* We will learn more about the dynamics and processes of resilience as research in the field continues and more literature becomes available.

Resilience and Pastoral Theology

The study and practice of resilience for pastoral leaders must find its foundation in the field of pastoral theology. Pastoral theology is biblical theology from a shepherding perspective. "Pastoral theology, then, properly relates to the interface between theology and Christian doctrine on the one hand, and pastoral experience and care on the other."[5] It is theology which must never be removed from the life of the Church.

Given this need to be grounded in pastoral theology, the study of resilience must include conversations with:

- biblical studies
- theological traditions
- spiritual formation
- pastoral counseling

These categories will be evident in the ten principles for resilience which are developed in this book.

4. Patterson and Kelleher, *Resilient School Leaders*, 3.
5. Tidball, *Skillful Shepherds*, 24.

Key Factors in Developing Pastoral Resilience

Developing pastoral leadership resiliency is an intentional process which incorporates key principles for personal growth in a holistic manner. It is not accomplished alone, but in community with others.

Developing pastoral resilience is not a linear process, but cyclical. The ten principles developed in this material are not a magic formula, but integral components of receiving God's grace and power for faithful and effective ministry leadership.

Recent Research on Themes for Pastoral Resilience

Bob Burns, Tasha Chapman, and Donald Guthrie conducted research for seven years focusing on gathering pastors and their spouses into peer cohorts and meeting in multiday retreats. These three individuals facilitated discussions about the challenges of ministry leadership. This study was funded through the Lilly Endowment's Sustaining Pastoral Excellence program. The following quote from the book which was written from this research summarizes their findings:

> After seven years of studying our summit participants—their personal lives, marriages, families, and ministries—we learned a lot about what it takes to survive and thrive in ministry. We spent hundreds of hours working through all of the data, pondering our notes and talking about our thoughts and reflections. Eventually our discoveries focused around five primary themes for leadership resilience in fruitful ministry:
>
> - spiritual formation
> - self-care
> - emotional and cultural intelligence
> - marriage and family
> - leadership and management[6]

6. Burns et al., *Resilient Ministry*, 16.

The next section will take a closer look at the biblical perspective on the subject of resilience.

A BIBLICAL PERSPECTIVE ON RESILIENCE (PERSEVERANCE)

The biblical term for resilience is "perseverance" or "patient endurance." It is the Greek word ὑπομονή. In the active sense it refers to "steady persistence in well-doing" and in the passive sense it is "patient endurance under difficulties."[7] Perhaps the best way to unpack the biblical perspective on the subject is to examine three different leaders in the early church.

Peter as Resilient Leader

Peter was introduced to Jesus by his brother Andrew. Both would later accept the call of Jesus to follow him and become fishers of men (Mark 1:16–20). Jesus would give him the name Cephas, which is the Aramaic word for "rock." Peter became a leader among the apostles and was in the inner circle of Jesus' followers, along with John and James.

Peter became a prominent figure in the gospel stories. His journey with Jesus was one filled with emotional encounters with others and with Jesus. His strong, impulsive personality is evident throughout the gospel narratives. His faith development is not a story of consistent, linear development, but one of great statements of faith mixed with miserable failures.

The darkest part of Peter's journey occurred the night of the arrest of Jesus in the garden of Gethsemane. In the courtyard of the high priest, Peter is confronted about his relationship with Jesus. He denies not only that he is a follower of Jesus, but denies that he even knows Jesus! "He disappointed himself, failed in his

7. cf. Brown, *Dictionary*, 772–776.

leadership role in the team, and, above all, dishonored the one who meant more to him than life itself."[8]

The restoration of this apostle is recorded in John 21. In this encounter with his risen Lord, Peter is not only forgiven, but given a charge to care for the spiritual lambs whom God would give him in the future. He is reinstated to a role of leadership among the apostles and in the founding of the church. The book of Acts reveals how Peter fulfilled his role and followed his Lord.

As Peter neared the end of his life, he wrote two letters to his flock which was scattered throughout Asia Minor. He wrote as a resilient pastor who has experienced much pain and suffering but has not lost his hope in the "God of all grace" (1 Pet 5:10). The maturity developed through a thirty-year journey of following his Lord through many victories and defeats is evident as he writes to them as a servant, an apostle, and a fellow elder with the elders among them. His life and words serve as an encouragement to believers to trust in the power of Jesus Christ as they face the challenges and persecution which will come their way because of their faith.

Peter's first letter is particularly instructive to leaders today who want to persevere in the midst of an ever-increasingly hostile culture. A portion of that letter reveals key aspects of character development and spiritual formation for the leader:

> *Humble* yourselves, therefore, under the mighty hand of God so that at the proper time he may exalt you, *casting all your anxieties on him*, because he cares for you. Be sober-minded; *be watchful*. Your adversary the devil prowls around like a roaring lion, seeking someone to devour. Resist him, *firm in your faith*, knowing that the same kinds of suffering are being experienced by your brotherhood throughout the world. And after you have suffered a little while, the God of all grace, who has called you to his eternal glory in Christ, will himself *restore, confirm, strengthen, and establish you*. To him be the dominion forever and ever. Amen.[9]

8. Howell, *Servants of the Servant*, 212.

9. 1 Peter 5:6–11. ESV.

Paul as Resilient Leader

The second great example of a resilient leader is the apostle Paul. This great apostle and missionary of the early church was born into a devout Jewish family in Tarsus, which was a leading city in the province of Cilicia. The fact that he was born and lived in Tarsus gave him many advantages which would later come to light in his leadership and church planting. He certainly was able to read and speak several languages, including Greek, Latin, Aramaic, and Hebrew.

As he developed through the years, Paul was zealous in his faith and a self-proclaimed "Hebrew of Hebrews" (Phil 3:5). The biblical account reveals that Paul was active in the persecution of the early Christians. His desire for an even greater level of persecution of Christians led him to travel to Damascus. While on this journey, Paul experienced an encounter with the resurrected Jesus that changed his life forever. His future would now be dedicated to serving Jesus.

After a period of approximately ten years,[10] Paul became a member of a team of leaders in the church at Antioch, the third largest city in the Roman empire. It was at Antioch that Paul and his friend Barnabas were set apart for the missionary/church-planting work which God had for them. For the last two decades of his life, Paul faithfully served his Lord by preaching, teaching, mentoring, and shepherding disciples of Christ.

Paul's many letters reveal the significant struggles and pain which he endured for the sake of the gospel. One of his most powerful personal testimonies about his ministry is found in 2 Corinthians 4:

> But we have this treasure in jars of clay, to show that the surpassing power belongs to God and not to us. We are afflicted in every way, but not crushed; perplexed, but not driven to despair; persecuted, but not forsaken; struck down, but not destroyed; always carrying in the body the death of Jesus, so that the life of Jesus may also

10. cf. Cole, *Journeys to Significance*, 29.

> be manifested in our bodies. For we who live are always being given over to death for Jesus' sake, so that the life of Jesus also may be manifested in our mortal flesh. So death is at work in us, but life in you. Since we have the same spirit of faith according to what has been written, "I believed, and so I spoke," we also believe, and so we also speak, knowing that he who raised the Lord Jesus will raise us also with Jesus and bring us with you into his presence. For it is all for your sake, so that as grace extends to more and more people it may increase thanksgiving to the glory of God.[11]

In one of his final letters, Paul uses three metaphors which provide for us a reinforcement of the truth that because of its challenges, ministry requires resilience:

> *I have fought the good fight, I have finished the race, I have kept the faith.* Henceforth, there is laid up for me the crown of righteousness, which the Lord, the righteous judge, will award to me on that Day, and not only to me but also to all who have loved his appearing.[12]

The resilient leader is one who finishes well. He or she may have many scars at the end of the journey, but there is a great sense of satisfaction in a life lived faithfully in honor to Jesus and in service to others.

James as Resilient Leader

His life's journey began in the same home as Jesus of Nazareth. According to many writers, he was the next oldest child of Mary and Joseph. He was raised in a godly home and was a devout follower of his faith. However, as Jesus began His public ministry, James was not in sympathy with the claims being made by Jesus. His conversion to become a follower of Jesus apparently did not occur until the resurrected Jesus appeared to him (1 Cor 15:7).

11. 2 Cor 4:7–15.

12. 2 Tim 4:7, 8.

James quickly became the recognized leader of the church in Jerusalem. Through the book of Acts and Paul's testimony about James, it is clear that he functioned as the primary leader in Jerusalem. Apparently, as one of the witnesses to the resurrection of Jesus and as a man of great faith and character, James became recognized as the leader in Jerusalem, especially as other leaders began to expand their ministries into new geographical areas.

The character and wisdom of this godly leader are particularly evident in the Jerusalem Council (Acts 15) and the crisis faced by the church. James exercises great wisdom and sensitivity as he takes the prominent role in this situation. He has a deep concern to "preserve the rights of both groups—Gentile Christians . . . and Jewish Christians."[13] His influence was recognized throughout the early church, particularly among the Jewish Christians.

James remained a faithful leader in the church for nearly thirty years. According to the writing of Josephus, he was stoned to death at the direction of the high priest, Ananus, for violating the Jewish laws. He remained faithful unto death in service to his Lord and the church.

It is in the writing of James that we are encouraged to persevere, and these words come from one who would persevere through many leadership challenges even unto martyrdom:

> Count it all joy, my brothers, when you meet trials of various kinds, for you know that *the testing of your faith produces steadfastness* (ὑπομονή). And let steadfastness have its full effect, that you may be perfect and complete, lacking in nothing.[14]

The lives and words of these three leaders reveal to us that resilience is a lifelong process which develops maturity in the faithful leader.

13. Thielman, *Theology of the New Testament*, 498.

14. James 1:2–4.

Some Final Thoughts on a Biblical Perspective on Resilience

The examples of Peter, Paul, and James reveal that life and leadership in the church are complex, costly, and filled with ambiguities. Serving as a leader of God's people often includes much heartache and pain. At the same time, the call to pastoral leadership is a call to a wonderful, fulfilling, and rewarding work. But it is a call not to be accepted lightly or naively. If one is to finish well, ministry must begin and end with God. It is about Him and His glory, not about me.

The goal in becoming a resilient pastor is to live and minister with others in ways that lead to vitality, joy, and growth *while* facing the adversities of ministry with a solid faith. We want to finish well in our ministry leadership, and this cannot happen accidentally.

As Paul challenged Timothy, may we devote ourselves to ministry even as we "keep a close watch on yourself and on the teaching. Persist in this, for by so doing you will save both yourself and your hearers" (1 Tim 4:15, 16).

STRUCTURE OF THE BOOK

The ten principles for developing pastoral resilience shared in this book have developed from my study of scripture, insights from my own leadership experiences, and insights from books and reflections by pastoral leaders. The book will include the sections listed below.

Narrative on the Ten Principles

Each chapter will address one of the ten principles which are key for developing pastoral resiliency. The material has been developed through: examination of biblical teaching and the lives of biblical leaders, insights from books on basic leadership principles, the author's own pastoral ministry experience of twenty-four years, the author's involvement in the leadership development of pastors and seminarians, and application of important counseling theories and practices.

Biblical Case Studies

Each principle will also be illustrated by examining the life of a biblical leader. Some of those to be included will be Moses, David, Nehemiah, Paul, and Timothy.

Testimonies of Experienced Pastors/Leaders

Each principle will be emphasized in a unique way through the testimony of an experienced pastor who has led a long-term ministry. The pastors will represent a variety of contexts and denominations. For example, one testimony will be from a Southern Baptist pastor who leads a mega-church. Another will be from a Congregational Christian pastor who serves in a small, rural church. Two will be from experienced pastors who now serve as professors in a seminary.

Practical Exercises for Self-Understanding and Growth

Exercises will be included within the body of the chapter or in appendices which will allow the reader to apply the principles which are being discussed. Many of these exercises will accomplish maximum benefit only when done with other leaders in a small group or one-on-one context.

Additional Resources

Suggestions will be provided in each chapter for other resources which may be utilized by the reader to go deeper in understanding each of the ten principles.

1

PRINCIPLE ONE

Develop Intimacy with God

Jason had served in three pastoral roles for the past 14 years. After graduating with high honors from a well-known evangelical seminary in the Midwest, he had accepted a call to the youth pastor position in a medium-sized church. His excitement for his new position was matched by his new bride. In every way, it was a rewarding ministry that led to broader recognition for Jason among other church leaders in his denomination. After four years, Jason accepted the position of discipleship pastor in a larger congregation. By this time, Jason and his wife were parents of two children and life had become much more hectic. Once again, Jason began his ministry with great excitement. It quickly became apparent that this new role and this new church were much more demanding of Jason's time and energy. His relationship with the senior pastor was positive, but mainly about the business of the ministry and not about relationships. Three years into this position, Jason realized that he was teaching others about discipleship and spiritual growth, but that he was personally not experiencing any growth or transformation. As he reflected upon his situation, he came to realize that even though he had taken a class on spiritual formation in seminary, he had never practiced the spiritual disciplines consistently, nor had he been mentored by anyone else in this area of his life. The way he was carrying out his ministry came from what he had read about, not what he had lived. Jason shared his uneasiness with his wife and together they prayed that God would bring someone into his life who would invest in his own spiritual formation. A few months later, at a pastors conference, Jason had a "chance meeting" with the pastor from a small rural church in his area. Their conversation quickly turned to the topic of discipleship, and Jason realized that here was someone who not only knew about spiritual formation, but had lived it for many years as he served faithfully in his pastoral role. They soon began meeting together, and Jason's spiritual growth took off. This relationship continued for the next three years, and Jason not only learned more about spiritual formation, but was being transformed from within. In his third and current ministry, which began four years ago, Jason is discipling his church members in vital spiritual growth and ministry.

Fortunately, at a critical point in his life and ministry, Jason recognized his spiritual dryness and that he was leading on empty spiritually. Even though he was "effective" in his ministry, he knew that he could not continue, or he would crash. God provided the right person at the right time for Jason. He learned the important principle that if one is to be a resilient pastor, he must seek and nourish intimacy with God.

Richard Foster's critique of our culture three decades ago is unfortunately also accurate of the state of leadership in the church today:

> Superficiality is the curse of our age. The doctrine of instant satisfaction is a primary spiritual problem. The desperate need today is not for a greater number of intelligent people, or gifted people, but for deep people.[1]

1. Foster, *Celebration of Discipline*, 1.

We need pastoral leaders in churches today who are deep people. This means that they have made a serious commitment to personal spiritual growth which is focused on a cooperative relationship with the Holy Spirit in a journey toward spiritual maturity.

Seeking a more intimate relationship with the Triune God requires surrender, focus, and commitment. It will demand some changes in attitudes and behaviors. However, care must be taken that these efforts do not degenerate into a legalistic attempt to earn God's love and acceptance. As Dallas Willard has noted, grace is opposed to earning, but not to effort.[2] As the apostle Paul challenged Timothy to "train yourself for godliness" (1 Tim 4:7), so will the resilient pastor seek spiritual vitality through intentionality, discipline, and perseverance.

HOLISTIC SPIRITUAL FORMATION

One of the dangers for Christian leaders is to separate one's practice of spiritual disciplines from other areas of spiritual growth. When this happens, it can result in a biblically anemic practice of one's faith or a "faith without works" spirituality or a belief that knowledge equals maturity. Another related danger is that the leader begins to practice a "check list" spirituality.

Figure 1 gives a simple depiction of what holistic spirituality involves. It can serve as a reminder of a broader perspective as we examine some of the specifics in developing a deeper intimacy with our Triune God.

Pastoral formation of Christian leaders must be viewed as spiritual formation from a holistic perspective. It is important to wed scholarship and spiritual passion for emerging leaders. Unfortunately, some seminaries and church leaders have developed a divide between theology and praxis. We need to work to restore the wedding of theology and praxis as was the model of the early church theologians. They were theologians *and* pastors. They knew

2. Willard, "Spiritual Formation," 7.

that good theology resulted in healthy ministry and that healthy ministry included good theology.

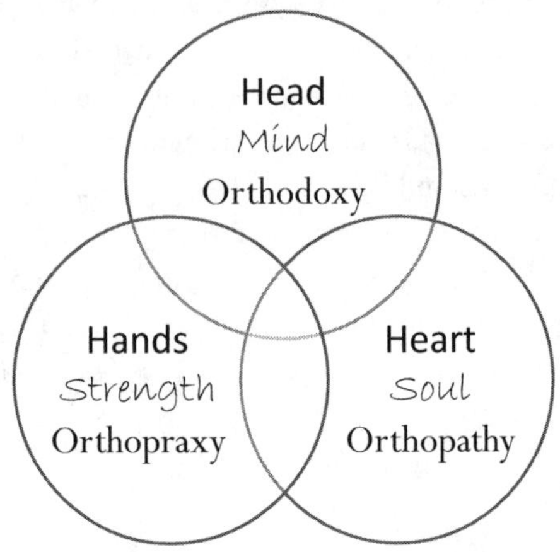

"You shall love the *Lord your God*

With all your *heart* and with all your *soul*

And with all your *mind* and with all your *strength*."

Spiritual formation is a Spirit-directed process

of being conformed to the image of Christ

in a holistic manner (soul, mind, and strength).

Three Daily Prayers

"Shape my heart" – Ps 51:10 and Ezek 36:26

"Renew my mind" – Rom 12:2

"Use my hands" – Col 3:23–24

OBSTACLES TO SPIRITUAL VITALITY

The enemy delights in distracting a Christian leader from the commitment to doing this inner work which provides a solid foundation for public ministry. The enemy wants leaders to focus on the "good" while neglecting the "best."

As I have experienced my own leadership ministries in the local church and in seminaries, I have observed ten major obstacles to spiritual vitality which are faced by leaders. This is not an exhaustive list, but certainly identifies many of the biggest obstacles.

1. *Complacency*—When living with and working with Scripture, prayer, and spiritual direction on a daily basis, it is easy to become complacent about one's own use of these spiritual tools in personal growth and development. For many seminarians, the Bible can become a book to be studied rather than the living word of God which brings conviction and comfort.
2. *Unresolved areas of sin and disobedience*—Hiding from or ignoring one's sin is a common danger for believers, especially for those who are expected to lead others. Unfortunately, many leaders do not have a healthy view or practice of confession as a spiritual discipline. Confession brings healing and empowers one for greater ministry.
3. *Legalism*—The tension of accepting the challenge of personal discipline versus a legalistic practice of spiritual activities is real. For those of us who were raised in families or traditions that tended toward "works righteousness," it can be an even more difficult challenge. The tendency is to practice Bible reading, prayer, etc. so we can check it off our list of things to do. It has been a continuing process in my own growth to practice intimacy with God with the focus on the relationship.
4. *Using service for Christ as an excuse for not spending time with Christ*—Pastors are busy leaders. There is a temptation to rationalize the fact that one is so busy with serving Christ by serving others that it is fine to miss consistent personal time with Christ.
5. *Focusing primarily on the need for blessings and neglecting the demands of discipleship*—One of the biggest challenges in the American church is the narcissistic society which permeates

everything. We tend to be more concerned about what we can receive from God, rather than what we can give to God.

6. *Substituting knowledge for relationship*—As a teacher and mentor of theological students, I must consistently emphasize that both head and heart are to be nourished. The greater temptation for most theological institutions is to elevate the cerebral aspects of spiritual formation above the heart aspects. For teachers and pastors, we must be careful not to promote a dichotomy which separates the two.
7. *Lack of awareness of the effects of past relational wounds*—The most significant community in our lives that shapes our view of God and our relationship with him is the family of origin. If one has experienced significant relational wounds from that community or other close people, the healing of those wounds is an important part of spiritual development. Failure to experience this healing can have a negative impact on intimacy with God.
8. *Misunderstanding of the value of suffering*—In our culture there is a view that suffering must be avoided at all costs. Therefore, it is to be medicated or anesthetized in some manner. For holistic spiritual growth, suffering must be viewed as part of God's desire to shape us.
9. *Belief that spiritual formation is only an individual matter*—As we observe the life of Jesus, we see that there were many times when he withdrew from others to be alone with the Father. But there were also other occasions in his life when prayer and focus on the Scriptures took place in community. Our intimacy with God is private, but also occurs in community with other believers.
10. *Distorted understanding of Scripture*—This obstacle points to the need for a solid understanding of the Word and the principles for understanding and interpreting it.

Any one of these obstacles can sidetrack a leader from an openness to the work of the Spirit as he seeks to bring about that work of transformation in the leader's inner life.

DAVID: A MAN AFTER GOD'S HEART

Israel's greatest king was not a man who was without sin in his life. But he was a man who pursued God and longed for intimacy with God, his Shepherd.

David's passion for Yahweh is revealed in the Scriptures through the psalms he wrote. These psalms have served as an inspiration for many believers who have used them for their own journeys with the Lord. In these psalms, there are models to follow for repentance, transparency, grief, and celebration. The range of emotions revealed in them provide a look into the soul of this man who was seeking God's heart:

- David invited God to search him and know him (Ps 139).
- David confessed his sin before God and prayed for forgiveness and cleansing (Ps 51).
- David declared the praise of God who delivered him from the pit of destruction, set his feet upon the rock, and put a new song in his mouth (Ps 40).
- David blessed the Lord at all times (Ps 34).
- David professed the need to be still before the Lord and to wait patiently upon him (Ps 37).
- David expressed his discouragement as his enemies sought to destroy him and asked the Lord to bring his judgment upon them (Ps 69).
- David expressed his deep trust in the Good Shepherd who provided for all his needs (Ps 23).

In David, we are able to see the journey of a flawed leader who valued his communion with God so deeply that he honestly and continually poured out his heart to God with no pretension. It was that communion with the living God which provided him the strength to face all his transgressions and enemies with confidence. David fully understood that God was his Redeemer and Shepherd!

RULE OF LIFE

Unfortunately, many Christian leaders are not intentional about developing a plan for their own spiritual development. Without such a focus, spiritual growth through intimacy with God doesn't happen, or at best, happens very haphazardly. The demands of life—family, job, commitments—quickly crowd out the time which needs to be spent with God.

One of the historic means of bringing order and intention to one's spiritual growth has been the "Rule of Life." The Rule of St. Benedict has been a model for many believers in many different traditions for many centuries. In the past few years, there has been a renewal of interest in teaching believers to develop a rule of life to bring order into their frazzled lives.[3]

"A rule of life is a pattern of spiritual disciplines that provides structure and direction for growth in holiness."[4] It is an intentional plan to keep the Triune God at the center of our life. The word *rule* can be threatening to many believers because it sounds like legalism.[5] The actual intention is to provide a plan that assists a believer in personal spiritual practices that bring about a deeper freedom, not to be more restrictive.

Knowing that many pastors and other Christian leaders will respond with thoughts like "yes, but ministry is so unpredictable, and there are so many demands on my time," I want to encourage

3. Three examples of authors who encourage this practice are: Peter Scazzero (*Emotionally Healthy Spirituality*), Marjorie Thompson (*Soul Feast*), and Adele Ahlberg Calhoun (*Spiritual Disciplines Handbook*).

4. Thompson, *Soul Feast*, 146.

5. The Latin term for "rule" is *regula* from which we get our words "regulate" and "regular." It also comes from the Greek word for "trellis" which has the intention to aid the growth and development of plants.

them not to write off this teaching about rule of life. Following will be practical suggestions which allow one to begin in a simple, small way in this practice. It can bring more freedom and fulfillment to your ministry. And I have found that it brings more peace in the midst of hectic weeks of leadership. The value of even five minutes spent in quiet and reflection in the middle of a day can be amazing.

The development of a rule of life is an act of intentionality in obeying the challenge which Paul gave to Timothy to "train yourself for godliness."[6] As Paul's use of the athletic analogy here shows, it requires discipline and effort.

Three Important Questions

Marjorie Thompson suggests that there are three basic questions that a Christian needs to ask in order to begin the process of developing a rule of life. Those questions are:

- What am I deeply attracted to, and why?
- Where do I feel God is calling me to stretch and grow?
- What kind of balance do I need in my life?[7]

After reflecting on these questions and listening to the leading of the Holy Spirit, one can begin to develop the priorities which should bring focus to the establishment of the rule of life. If you have never practiced following a rule of life, it is best to begin with a few commitments (three or four) rather than an extensive list.

Another suggestion is to consider seriously one's personality style and current life situation when developing the plan. Be realistic about your best times emotionally and about your life demands. For instance, if you currently have small children in your home, you will need to adjust your plan to their schedules and demands. If this is a particularly demanding time in your ministry, be realistic about how much you can begin now.

6. 1 Tim 4:7.

7. Thompson, *Soul Feast*, 150.

The Process and Elements of Developing a "Rule of Life"

Since the purpose of a rule of life is to keep the Triune God at the center of all of our life, it needs to have a holistic perspective. It will include disciplines that help form our heart, head, and hands.

There is no perfect model of a rule of life. However, there are many examples which can assist in the process of developing one's own rule. While considering other examples, the leader must give consideration to his or her own personality, temperament, strengths, calling, location, and stage of life. These factors will be a part of the reflection process as you consider Thompson's questions listed above. In addition, a rule of life is something to be reevaluated regularly (at least annually) and adjusted according to needs and growth.

Once you have developed your own personal rule of life, write it down and keep a copy where you can view it regularly (I keep mine in the front of my planner). Then, share your rule with someone whom you trust and ask that person to pray for your discipline and to keep you accountable.

Peter Scazzero suggests twelve elements for a personal rule of life.[8] These are all important areas of a leader's life, but this might be too much for many individuals. I would suggest beginning with the eight areas shown in the example below.

RULE OF LIFE

Vision: I will use my gifts and energy to recruit, teach, mentor, and encourage students who desire to grow in Christ and desire to serve him through his church.

Focus Scripture: "Him we proclaim, warning everyone and teaching everyone with all wisdom, that we may present everyone mature in Christ. For this I toil, with all his energy that he powerfully works within me." (Col 1:28–29)

8. Scazzero, *Emotionally Healthy Spirituality*, 199–207.

Scripture

- † Utilize the Bible reading plan of Robert Murray McCheyne
- † Specific study of Pastoral Epistles, utilizing Greek text and commentaries

Prayer and Solitude

- † Practice one-hour in one sitting of prayer and meditation two times per week
- † Use the prayers of John Baille for evening prayer with my wife (Linda)

Daily Office

- † Morning prayer focus using *Daily Affirmations*
- † Noon: 5 minutes of silence and prayer
- † Evening prayer from personal journal

Rest and Recreation

- † Take half day on Saturday or Sunday afternoon
- † Get 7 hours of sleep each night

Personal Care

- † Give attention to diet
- † Utilize exercise regimen four times per week
- † Process emotional state with Linda weekly

Family

- † Invest time daily to share with Linda
- † Communicate with (adult) sons on weekly basis

Ministry/Service

- † Fulfill role of elder at MBCC
- † Give 2–3 hours per month for service project

Community

- † Encourage colleagues
- † Monthly meeting with mentor

This rule of life example is unique to my personal situation currently. I regularly examine it and adjust as needed, considering feedback from my wife and from my mentor. This example may be used as a template, but the specifics may vary widely for different individuals.

As you begin your commitment to using a rule of life, take some time to pray and reflect upon this before writing your first draft. After discussing your draft with your mentor or a trusted spiritual friend, then make an initial commitment to practice this rule for at least six months. Keep in mind that the rule is not intended to add guilt, but to bring greater peace and freedom to your life. When you experience some failures, begin anew.

SPIRITUAL DISCIPLINES

Discipline has become an unpopular term in our culture. Even in some specific areas of our culture which formerly prized discipline (e.g., athletics), it seems that it has declined as a core value. Instant fulfillment of our desires has replaced this value.

Bible scholar and author, Dr. M. Robert Mulholland, provides a balanced view of the value and importance of the spiritual disciplines in our journey with the Triune God:

> Somewhere between the extremes of avoidance of discipline and the imprisonment of discipline is the holistic practice of balanced spiritual disciplines which become a means of God's grace to shape us in the image of Christ for others . . . Holistic spiritual disciplines are acts of loving obedience that we offer to God steadily and consistently, to be used for whatever work God purposes to do in and through our lives.[9]

The classic spiritual disciplines provide a framework for us to consider as we seek to go deeper in our journey with God. While some of these may be new for many leaders, it is important to

9. Mulholland, *Invitation to a Journey*, 103.

consider them even if one does not develop a particular discipline into a "holy habit."

Two different perspectives in viewing and utilizing these disciplines are found in Richard Foster's *Celebration of Discipline* and in Dallas Willard's *The Spirit of the Disciplines*. Foster divides the disciplines into three categories:

1. Inward Disciplines: Meditation, Prayer, Fasting, Study
2. Outward Disciplines: Simplicity, Solitude, Submission, Service
3. Corporate Disciplines: Confession, Worship, Guidance, Celebration

Willard divides the disciplines into two categories:

1. Disciplines of Abstinence: Solitude, Silence, Fasting, Frugality, Chastity, Secrecy, Sacrifice
2. Disciplines of Engagement: Study, Worship, Celebration, Service, Prayer, Fellowship, Confession, Submission

Both of these models contain value. The Christian leader who is committed to personal growth will take time to learn about the spiritual disciplines, practice them (experiment with them), and seek the guidance of the Holy Spirit in adding the practice of them to one's rule of life in a manner that is life-producing and not life-killing.

Both of these authors have many books which give biblical support, definitions, and practical advice to Christians who want to engage the disciplines on a deeper level. Other books will be suggested as well at the end of this chapter.

LYLE DORSETT: KNOWING CHRIST BETTER, LOVING HIM MORE

The apostle John wrote that the Lord Jesus Christ prayed these words to his heavenly Father: "And this is eternal life, that they may know you, the only true God, and Jesus Christ whom you have sent" (John 17:3, NASB). I must confess that in the years immediately following my conversion, "eternal life"—to my mind—would begin at the moment of death when I enter paradise with the Lord. But several years later, the Lord brought a mentor into my life who helped me understand that eternal life begins the moment Christ enters the soul at conversion and that we grow in knowledge of him as our intimacy with him increases. In brief, the desire of every Christian should be to increasingly know Jesus better and love him more. Perhaps we can grasp this concept of intimacy by looking at marriage. My wife and I married over forty years ago. To be sure, we gained a certain level of intimacy at the outset of our marriage, but deeper and richer intimacy has increased through the years of sharing joys and sorrows together. Our intimacy has grown as we have purposively sought to serve and listen to each other and celebrate one another's attributes. And so it is with our Lord Jesus—our groom. In the church we are the bride of Christ, and we will only grow in deep and transformational intimacy when we seek to know Him.

We must choose to know him better and love him more. Daily disciplines I have found helpful are:

1. Begin my day praising Him—singing a verse or two of a praise hymn like "Holy, Holy, Holy" or "All Hail the Power of Jesus' Name" because Psalm 22:3 reveals that he indwells our praises.
2. Read the Bible, prayerfully seeking to hear him.
3. Set aside time to be alone with him in prayer just like he continually did with his Father in heaven.
4. Confess sins and pray Psalm 51: "create in me a clean heart and renew a right spirit within me."
5. At the end of each day, I thank God for ten good things that have happened. Indeed, at night my wife and I hold hands, and we each thank God for ten things. Thus we

end the day with thankful hearts regardless of how difficult the day might have been.

6. Finally, besides disciplines, I grow closer to Christ by being part of a local church where I can serve and be served.

These are a few things that have helped me know Jesus better and love Him more.

SOME THOUGHTS FOR EMERGING LEADERS

† Spiritual vitality is about a relationship. It is a living relationship with Jesus Christ that becomes a source of joy for the believer. Jesus describes the absolute necessity of this relationship in John 15. It is the focus of spiritual formation.

† The historical spiritual disciplines of the church "allow us to place ourselves before God so that He can transform us."[10] We must seek to practice these disciplines on a regular basis and to devote the time it takes to nurture this relationship with Jesus. As with any relationship, time is a necessary ingredient if there is to be any depth in the relationship. This relationship with Jesus will bring about transformation of one's thinking, feeling, and acting.

† Study and preparation for sermons and lessons is to be offered as an act of worship to God, but does not replace the need for reading and applying Scripture for oneself. One suggestion that has been beneficial to me is to use a different translation (at least occasionally) for one's personal reading.

† Spending 24–48 hours at least twice per year for a time of personal retreat and renewal is vital. This is best accomplished by going to a retreat center or abbey.

† It is essential to have a mentor in your life who regularly asks you, "How is your soul?"

10. Foster, *Celebration of Discipline*, 6.

ADDITIONAL RESOURCES

Benner, David G. *The Gift of Being Yourself.* Downers Grove, IL: InterVarsity, 2004.

Dorsett, Lyle W. *Seeking the Secret Place.* Grand Rapids, MI: Brazos, 2004.

Hudson, Trevor. *Discovering Our Spiritual Identity.* Downers Grove, IL: InterVarsity, 2010.

Mulholland, M. Robert. *Shaped By The Word.* Nashville, TN: Upper Room Books, 2000.

Nouwen, Henri J. *The Way of the Heart.* New York: Ballantine, 1981.

Ortberg, John. *Soul Keeping.* Grand Rapids, MI: Zondervan, 2014.

Sittser, Gerald L. *Water from a Deep Well.* Downers Grove, IL: InterVarsity, 2007.

Wilhoit, James C. *Spiritual Formation as if the Church Mattered.* Grand Rapids, MI: Baker Academic, 2008.

Willard, Dallas. *Renovation of the Heart.* Colorado Springs, CO: NavPress, 2002.

2

PRINCIPLE TWO

Invest in Mentoring Relationships

He was talented, successful, well-liked, and in demand as a speaker and seminar leader. The church he had planted had experienced rapid growth, and he now led a staff of four other pastors. Why did he need anyone in his life who would give him counsel and advice? Wasn't he the "mentor" to other young pastors?

His weekly schedule was always packed with appointments or travel to speaking engagements. He communicated clearly and passionately to those who attended the seminars. Many young church planters considered him to be the "expert" and often contacted him after seminars to seek advice and encouragement.

The event that brought him to a time of personal evaluation and deep reflection happened at the conclusion of one of his speaking engagements. It had been a particularly stressful month in his ministry, his youngest child had recently been diagnosed with ADHD, and his wife shared with him that she was feeling distance between them. After his last message at the conference, a young church planter who was obviously discouraged came to him and asked, "Jim, who is your pastor? Who mentors you and keeps you on track? I really need someone like that."

These questions hit Jim like a brick. He knew the true answer was "no one." Suddenly, he felt almost desperate, knowing that in this particularly difficult time in his life and ministry, there was no one to whom he could turn as a pastor or mentor. He realized how much he had been giving and how little he had been receiving. He knew that his life was out of balance and that his family was suffering and that there was no person in his life who held him accountable or who poured wisdom and counsel into him.

On the flight home that day, Jim confessed to his Lord and made a decision to live differently. He decided to take the next day to spend extended time with his wife to discuss what he had discovered, ask her forgiveness, and begin to plan to live a more balanced life which would include regular meetings with a mentor.

I met recently with a Christian leader of a parachurch ministry who is in his mid-40s. He and I have been meeting together consistently for almost four years. He calls me "coach." Our relationship is a mentoring relationship. As we prepared to depart, he asked me if I have someone in my life who is a mentor. My immediate response was "yes." We meet monthly, and his wisdom, counsel, and encouragement are invaluable to me. Over the past thirty-six years I have been in one-on-one or small group mentoring. I have had a variety of mentors. My longest intensive mentoring relationship with a mentor was four years; we usually met monthly. It is my conviction and plan to have a mentor throughout the rest of my life.

Paul Stanley and J. Robert Clinton completed a major study of leaders in which they discovered five characteristics of leaders who "finish well." One of those characteristics was "they had a network of meaningful relationships and several important mentors during their lifetime."[1] These mentors were able to listen,

1. Stanley and Clinton, *Connecting*, 215.

encourage, challenge, and provide accountability for these leaders. The importance of having a mentor and being involved in a constellation of mentoring relationships (described below) cannot be overemphasized.

THE MENTORING CONSTELLATION

The presence of mentors throughout a leader's journey has been shown to be one of the keys to meaningful and effective leadership over the long haul. But this involvement with mentors needs to be expanded to include not just being mentored, but also being a mentor to others.

The term which I will use to describe this involvement is the "mentoring constellation." I first encountered this term in Stanley and Clinton's work, *Connecting*. However, I have found that the origin of the use of the term is from the work of Kathy Kram.[2]

Many leaders fail to realize the importance of being involved in such a network of relationships until they have experienced a serious ministry or moral failure or until they are extremely discouraged. My encouragement to emerging leaders is that they view their involvement in these relationships as an investment in their lives and ministries. The diagram below (Figure 2) shows four different relationships for the pastoral leader to include in a personal network. Each will be described briefly.

Mentor: Each leader will benefit from an ongoing relationship with a mentor. The mentor is an individual who is respected for spiritual maturity, life experience, wisdom, and particular skill set. The particularities of the relationship will be addressed later (content, agendas, schedule, etc.).

Protégé: Each leader will discover the rewards in being a mentor by serving in that role for a protégé who views him or her as that mature, wise individual who can invest in the protégé's development. Serving as a mentor will provide an opportunity to invest in the development of future kingdom leaders.

2. Cf. Kram, *Mentoring at Work*.

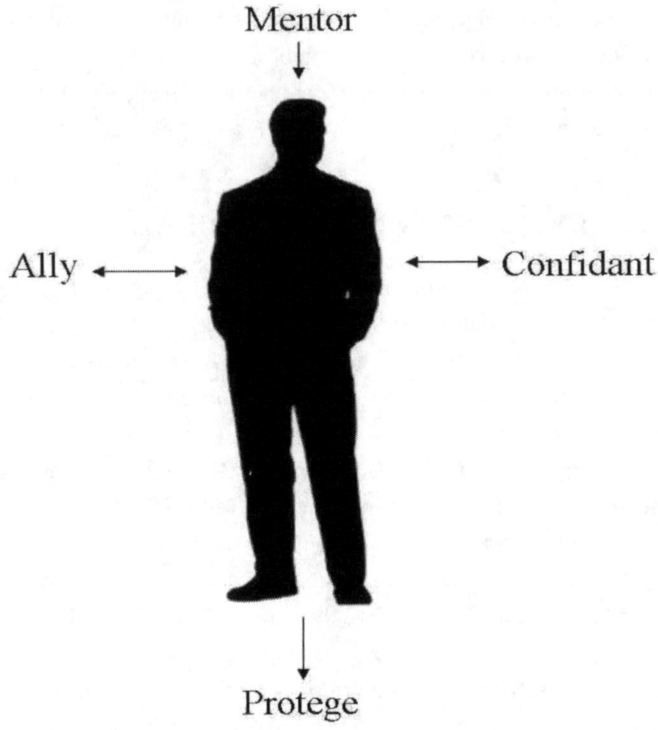

Ally: Peer mentoring relationships are part of this constellation. The "ally" is called an "internal peer mentor" by Stanley and Clinton.[3] An ally is an individual within your leadership organization with whom you meet regularly to process what is transpiring within the organization.

Confidant: A "confidant" is called an "external peer mentor."[4] This person is someone who is a peer, but not within your organizational structure. The confidant becomes a trusted friend who will speak truth into your life and has no competing loyalties with the organization.

The concept of the mentoring constellation can be intimidating, especially if one begins to consider what this might mean in terms of time investment. So, the first question to answer is

3. Stanley and Clinton, *Connecting*, 189.

4. Ibid.

"How can I possibly be involved in this many different mentoring relationships?"

Not all of these relationships require a weekly, or even monthly, investment of time. However, it could add up to four or five hours per month to one's schedule. You are encouraged to meet monthly with your mentor (1½–2 hours), monthly with your protégé (1½–2 hours), and every four to six weeks with your peer mentors (1 hour). It will be important to evaluate what can be deleted from one's schedule to make the time for these important relationships. This will happen only if there is a strong commitment to mentoring as a part of one's leadership development.

The second question to answer is "Why should I make this time in my busy schedule?" My first answer is because it was the model of Jesus. He invested most of his time in a small group of followers who would carry on his mission after his departure. The second reason is that it will result in a deeper life for you, your protégé/s, and your peers. Also, it will strengthen you as you face the inevitable challenges and conflicts of leadership.

PAUL AND TIMOTHY: MENTOR & PROTÉGÉ

The apostle Paul invested himself in other faithful servants of God who were willing to make a commitment to God's call and purpose in their lives. In Paul's thirteen letters, we find the names of many individuals (more than 100) whom he discipled and *mentored*, serving alongside them in ministry.

One of Paul's most significant protégés was Timothy. Timothy left his home in Lystra to join Paul and Silas on their missionary journey (Acts 16:1–5), and throughout the rest of Paul's life, Timothy was either Paul's companion or his emissary. Paul considered Timothy to be his "true child in the faith."[5]

Paul mentored Timothy as they ministered together. Timothy was able to witness directly Paul's teaching, preaching,

5. 1 Tim 1:2

witnessing, confronting, and suffering as he planted new churches and directed their ministries. Through his mentor's example, Timothy could learn about Christian resilience and ministry on a very practical level.

While Timothy would learn much from his spiritual father's letters to him, he gained many invaluable lessons from serving alongside him:

- † the Scriptures provide the foundation for teaching
- † suffering for Christ will be part of leadership ministry
- † young believers need continual teaching and discipling
- † a mentor will be concerned about the physical and spiritual needs
- † empowering a protégé includes giving direct responsibilities

Paul was a faithful mentor to Timothy, and he encouraged him to pass the baton of faith to others who would then mentor others (2 Tim 2:2)

BASIC TYPES OF MENTORING

The concept of mentoring has been defined in many ways by many different authors. In recent years, mentoring has been the subject of much research in various fields, and many dissertations have been written on this subject. There appears to be no universal definition for mentoring, and in the past decade, new distinctions have been made between "mentoring" and "coaching."

Here I provide my operational definition for mentoring:

> Mentoring is a voluntary, intensive relationship in which a mentor empowers a protégé by sharing God-given resources in an intentional manner.

Various implications and applications of this definition will be described in other portions of the chapter.

Although the word "mentor" does not appear in the Bible, there are many images in Scripture which provide biblical support for this concept. I provide a detailed description and application of these images in chapters one and two of *The Ministry of Mentoring*.[6] As we look to Jesus as our example for mentoring, we read in the gospels that the primary terms utilized for this relationship are "master/teacher" and "disciple." The master would teach and mold the disciples as they lived life together. While mentoring relationships today are not typically carried out with such an intense living arrangement, the value of mentoring experiences for such teaching and molding is still relevant.

Five Crucial Dynamics

Before discussing various types of mentoring, it is important to understand some crucial dynamics which are necessary for the mentoring experience to be most effective.

1. Compatibility—This is the beginning of the mentoring process; the mentor and protégé are drawn to each other as they see the potential in the relationship. Selecting a mentor (or protégé) is an important act, as the experience will shape each of the participants in the future. Beginning the selection process with a sense of affinity with the person being approached will be a positive step in the development of the overall experience.
2. Relationship—While this may sound redundant, it is important to note that the mentor and protégé must develop a relationship which extends beyond a mere communication of knowledge. The protégé is not simply a passive recipient of the wisdom of the "great teacher," but is a full participant in the process.
3. Responsiveness—The protégé must have an attitude of receptivity to the modeling and teaching of the mentor. This does not mean that the mentor must always have all the answers,

6. Searby, *The Ministry of Mentoring*. See also Appendix One for a brief summary.

or be seen as the final authority on every issue, but it does assume a willingness to listen and learn.

4. Accountability—Accountability is an important aspect of personal spiritual development for any Christian. It is particularly important for developing leaders who want to become models for others in the future. I believe that in the mentoring relationship, accountability should be viewed as helping another person keep personal commitments to God. This means that the mentor will help the protégé form those commitments, but ultimately the protégé must develop them. The protégé then gives permission to the mentor to hold him or her accountable.
5. Empowerment—Empowering other people means to help them to recognize their potential within and to encourage the development of that potential. Unfortunately, many protégés come into the mentoring relationship with a tremendous amount of baggage from their past history which has stifled their growth and clouds their self-perception. The mentor can assist the protégé in recognizing and embracing his or her potential and in developing a plan to build upon those strengths.

Types of Mentoring

I use the term "mentoring" as an umbrella term for various aspects of personal and leadership development. Underneath this umbrella are six types of mentoring which vary in intensity and style. These six are taken from a longer list developed by Paul Stanley and Robert Clinton in *Connecting*.

Mentor Role	**Major Focus**
Discipler	Enablement in the basics of the faith
Spiritual Guide	Acccountability for spiritual growth and practices

Coach	Help to facilitate greater skills and motivation
Counselor	Give perspective, advice on view of self and others
Teacher	Impart knowledge, conceptual insights, wisdom
Sponsor	Provide career guidance and protection

Here is a brief description of each type:

Discipler

One of the greatest needs in the church today is the training and equipping of new believers in the basics of their faith and in understanding the biblical demands of discipleship. It is a sad fact that many new Christians are never discipled in a systematic manner. The result is that many never get out of the spiritual nursery, or many leave the church after a few years. In my survey of seminarians each semester in my leadership class, it is typical that 75 percent or more were never mentored/discipled in this manner. Most received this type of mentoring later in life as college students involved in university ministries or at a Bible college.

There is a tremendous need for men and women who will fulfill this mentoring role of discipler. Mature Christian leaders can provide a significant ministry in churches by taking one or a small group of new Christians and teaching and discipling them as they begin their journey in the faith. This is a need for new Christians of all ages, not just youth.

There is an abundance of available materials which these mentors can use to disciple these believers. Each denomination typically has materials from its own publishing house which can provide a good beginning point, or books like *Discipleship Essentials* by Greg Ogden can be utilized.

Spiritual Guide

This basic type of mentoring carries a high level of accountability. The protégé asks the spiritual guide to keep him or her accountable for the practice of the spiritual disciplines and overall spiritual growth. The mentor will assist the protégé in evaluating his or her spiritual condition and provide guidance, primarily by asking probing questions. The mentor should be able to provide resources and ideas for spiritual growth for the protégé.

I have found it extremely valuable to have a mentor who functions as a "spiritual guide." My expectation is not that he is an expert in the spiritual disciplines, but that he is willing to hold me accountable in a healthy manner. This accountability includes a regular time of asking about the practice of the spiritual disciplines as well as a time of praying for my growth in this area. Since growth in prayer and the other disciplines has applications for relationships as well, these relationships are part of the accountability.

Coach

This type of mentoring has its main focus on skill development. The mentor who is functioning in this role will help the protégé increase skills and take practical steps toward goals. The coach may not be an expert in the protégé's particular field. This is not a requirement. However, it is important that the coach has leadership experience and an understanding of basic organizational principles.

In my current role as a "coach" to one of my protégés, we examine big picture items (e.g., personal mission, spiritual life, family issues), and I also help him to reflect on more specific items related to budgets, recruiting, and so on. This example reveals why I do not seek to make a strong differentiation between mentoring and coaching. I believe there is much overlap.[7]

7. In his book, *Christian Coaching*, Gary Collins defines coaching as "the art and practice of enabling individuals and groups to move from where they are to where they want to be." This definition has implications for many aspects

Counselor

The pastoral leader is always in need of a mentor who can provide clear and objective feedback on self-perception, especially in relationship to others. Self-understanding is crucial to becoming a healthy leader who leads oneself well and builds strong relationships with others. This concept will be fully developed later.

It is important to provide a disclaimer here. This type of mentoring should not be confused with "therapist." A therapist is an individual with specific cognitive and clinical training in order to provide therapy for an individual, couple, or family. Therapy involves a deeper psychological perspective for the client. If the mentor or protégé in a mentoring relationship perceives that therapy would be beneficial, then a referral needs to be made to a trained therapist/licensed counselor. For example, I have had protégés who have been in therapy as they were involved in regular mentoring sessions with me.

Teacher

The central focus of a teacher–mentor is to impart knowledge to the protégé on the topic which has been requested. The content of these mentoring sessions will be very focused, but need not ignore the more relational aspects of mentoring. As the mentor provides specific content and related resources for the protégé to use, the sessions can also serve to motivate the protégé for upcoming tasks. It is not unusual for this type of mentoring to be more limited in the number of sessions together or irregular in the frequency of the meetings.

---

of the protégé's life, including personal, spiritual, and professional. This is one reason why I use the term "mentoring" for this broad-based perspective and "coaching" in a more specific sense. For a comprehensive presentation on coaching, see Collins, *Christian Coaching*.

Sponsor

This type of mentoring has been very common in the corporate world. The mentor serves as a sponsor to provide specific career guidance with an intention to assist the protégé toward promotion within the organization. The agreement between mentor and protégé in this type of mentoring needs to be very clear and specific. Expectations must be fully disclosed and discussed.

Application of this specific type of mentoring relationship will vary greatly. In Christian organizations, particularly churches, the mentor will more commonly serve as a resource to help the protégé connect to other churches or organizations rather than providing support for promotion within the organization.

UNDERSTANDING THE PROCESS

For many years, I have taught seminary students the basic principles of mentoring and have also conducted many seminars about mentoring. It is rewarding to observe the excitement which builds in individuals as they begin to grasp the principles and see the potential for themselves and for their churches or organizations. However, I always include the admonition that the next step in the process is to spend time in prayer—prayer about the process, potential mentor or protégé, and one's own willingness to invest in the mentoring process.

Incidental or Intentional?

Mentoring in informal ways occurs every day and in many different ways. Many of us have experienced spontaneous mentoring, either as a mentor or protégé. While there is value in such informal encounters, what I am advocating in this book is an intentional plan to find and maintain healthy, productive mentoring relationships. You are encouraged to deliberately develop this ministry in order to develop other leaders as well as experience personal growth for yourself.

Quality mentoring relationships do not happen automatically. They take serious consideration, planning, nurturing, and evaluation. The example of Jesus, the Master Mentor, reveals to us that he had a "plan"[8] and that he was very intentional in the manner in which he developed his protégés.

The next portion of this chapter will provide two different frameworks for approaching the mentoring process in an intentional manner. While there will be some overlap, the desire is that any such redundancy will serve to reinforce critical pieces of the process. There are several other models which are useful and could have been utilized. The two I have chosen have been found to provide helpful, practical ideas for implementing mentoring relationships in one-on-one or group contexts.

ZACHARY'S FOUR-STAGE MENTORING CYCLE[9]

Lois Zachary is an internationally recognized expert in the field of mentoring. Three of her books—*The Mentor's Guide, Creating a Mentoring Culture,* and *The Mentee's Guide*—have been constant companions to me the past several years as I have studied the topic and developed workshops, seminars, and materials for groups and organizations. These books provide many practical exercises and inventories which can be utilized in the various phases of the mentoring process.

Zachary has presented a model for mentoring relationships which sets out four phases or stages. These stages are: "(1) preparing (getting ready), (2) negotiating (establishing agreements), (3) enabling (doing the work), and (4) coming to closure (integrating

8. Cf. Coleman, *The Master Plan of Evangelism.*

9. Zachary, *The Mentor's Guide.*

learning and moving forward)."[10] An understanding of this model is important for mentors and protégés who want to enter into effective mentoring relationships which provide meaningful interaction for both parties.

Preparing (Getting Ready)

One mistake made by many highly motivated individuals is to begin a mentoring relationship based upon one's enthusiasm and conviction without any preparation. Potential mentors and protégés need to give significant time and thought to the mentoring process *prior* to establishing an agreement. Giving this time and thought is the practice of reflection.

Personal reflection on how one has been shaped by past personal relationships and experiences is a good place to begin the preparation phase.[11] Next, it is helpful to reflect upon your current skills and to evaluate which are strengths and which are weaknesses. The reflection process should include spending time considering your goals. What would you like to accomplish in the next six months, year, and five years? In an ultimate way, this reflection should include consideration of Howard Hendricks's question posed at a Promise Keepers conference, "What am I doing today that will guarantee my impact for Jesus Christ in the next generation?"

The next task in the preparation phase is to consider what kind of mentor you need or what kind of protégé you will select. The potential intensity of mentoring relationships makes this selection crucial. We must choose our mentors and protégés wisely because these become significant shaping relationships in our lives. This aspect of the process also must be given sufficient time. "A substantial body of research finds that mentors and protégés

10. Zachary, *The Mentee's Guide*, 7.

11. Zachary has a very helpful template in *The Mentee's Guide* to assist with this process, 19. There are many other templates provided in her book which can assist the mentor and protégé in this entire process, as indicated in subsequent footnotes.

who are well matched on important personal and professional dimensions form stronger, more enduring, and more beneficial relationships."[12]

Zachary has a helpful chart[13] which provides a model for making a decision about mentor selection. The steps are listed below:

Step 1: Identify your goal

Step 2: Create a list of criteria

Step 3: Determine qualities that are "musts"

Step 4: Rank the remaining criteria ("wants") in order of importance

Step 5: List the possible options

Step 6: Eliminate options that don't meet the "musts"

Step 7: Rate each option against "wants"

Step 8: Make the decision

Utilizing these steps can be very helpful in the selection process for a mentor or protégé. However, it is absolutely crucial to remember that the entire process must begin and end with prayer, and be bathed in prayer throughout. After essentially utilizing this process in the past, I took an additional three months to pray and listen for God's leading in my selection of my mentor. It is that crucial to have the leading and confirmation of the Holy Spirit in this process!

The final aspect of the preparation phase is ready to be initiated. It is time to have the initial mentoring conversation. Zachary's template[14] is very thorough in providing the main topics which need to be included in this conversation.

Negotiating (Establishing Agreements)

One of the biggest obstacles to effective mentoring relationships is a lack of clarity about the expectations and ground rules for the

12. Johnson and Ridley, *The Elements of Mentoring*, 64.

13. Zachary, *The Mentee's Guide*, 40.

14. Zachary, *The Mentee's Guide*, 50.

relationship. The establishment of agreements prior to entering into the relationship can prevent most misunderstandings and help focus the mentoring experience.

Adapted from Zachary's work, here are five crucial ingredients in the development of a covenant agreement for the mentoring relationship:

1. Goals: What do I want to learn/gain through this relationship?
2. Ground Rules: What are the guidelines for meetings, and who is responsible?
3. Confidentiality: What level of confidentiality is assumed in our meetings?
4. Boundaries: What is appropriate and inappropriate in our relationship[15]
5. Addressing Differences: How will confrontation be addressed?

This phase is not complete until a written covenant has been drafted and signed by both parties. This document provides a "map" for the relationship and a tool for evaluation and closure.

Enabling (Doing the Work)

"This is the time in a mentoring relationship during which you execute the work of mentoring, strengthen your relationship, and make tangible progress toward your mentoring goals, guided by your established agreements."[16] Most of the growth in the mentoring relationship occurs during this phase, and it is the longest of the four phases.

Effective mentoring relationships find a balance in developing the relationship on a personal level while working toward the agreed upon learning goals. In healthy, warm mentoring

15. Johnson and Ridley provide a list of important boundary issues to cover in *The Elements of Mentoring*.

16. Zachary, *The Mentee's Guide*, 79.

relationships, it is important that both parties discipline themselves to focus on the goals and not allow the relationship to become only a good time of social interaction. Regular evaluation of the relationship is imperative.

One tool that can be helpful to both mentor and protégé is a journal. Each can record his perception of the session and what was accomplished, then this can be utilized to review the previous session and assist with planning for future sessions.

The learning goals of the protégé will carry significant weight in the content of these ongoing sessions. The goals may be strong in content, relationship, or some other aspect of development. The basic type of the relationship (e.g., counselor, coach) also will help determine the content and tone of the sessions.

Coming to Closure (Integrating Learning and Moving Forward)

This is the mentoring phase in which you reflect on what you have learned during your mentoring relationship and position yourself to continue the momentum of your own developmental journey long after the relationship is over. . . . Coming to closure also allows you to redefine the relationship and comfortably move on.[17]

This may not be the end of your mentoring relationship with a particular individual, but rather a time to close an agreed-upon chapter and make plans to move ahead. In one of my mentoring relationships, my mentor and I had agreed upon a time of one year, meeting monthly. After one year, we evaluated the relationship and agreed to meet for another year. In the end, we met for four years consecutively.

Closure is one aspect of mentoring relationships which is often neglected. This can result in hurt feelings or great disappointment if not handled correctly. Zachary's template[18] provides

17. Ibid., 99.

18. Zachary, *The Mentee's Guide*, 109.

the core elements for closure and specific questions to process together.

STANLEY AND CLINTON'S "TEN COMMANDMENTS OF MENTORING"

The second set of guidelines which are helpful in developing and maintaining healthy mentoring relationships is the "Ten Commandments of Mentoring"[19] developed by Paul Stanley and Robert Clinton. They simply will be listed below (see the pages indicated in the footnote for a fuller description of each).

1. Establish the mentoring relationship.
2. Jointly agree on the purpose of the relationship.
3. Determine the regularity of interaction.
4. Determine the type of accountability.
5. Set up communication mechanisms.
6. Clarify the level of confidentiality.
7. Set the life cycle of the relationship.
8. Evaluate the relationship periodically.
9. Modify expectations to fit the real life context.
10. Bring closure to the mentoring experience.

There are several areas in which Stanley and Clinton agree with Zachary. Both of these resources provide helpful information to those who want to begin a mentoring relationship or equip others to be involved in a ministry of mentoring.

In spite of the resistance by some toward formalizing the mentoring relationship as encouraged by these authors, I believe that there is greater potential for good things to happen and less chance for bad things to happen in these relationships whenever

19. Stanley and Clinton, *Connecting*, 197–208.

the mentor and protégé have invested in this type of intentional process.

DICK WAMSLEY: LIFE MENTORS

Growing up with an alcoholic father, my need for male mentors was critical in my formative years. During college and seminary, two incidental mentors reinforced my growing confidence and helped to elevate my self-esteem. One was a peer and the other a professor. My peer and closest friend was a gifted leader who was loaded with self-confidence. He helped me pursue possibilities for ministry I would have never considered on my own, resulting in my taking on a weekend preaching ministry at a small church at age nineteen.

The professor took me aside one day after an Abnormal Psychology class and told me I had good insights into human behavior in class discussions. He encouraged me to pursue studies in the field of psychology and counseling. That informal encounter led me to complete two masters degrees, one in pastoral counseling and one in student personnel work in higher education. That professor became a lifelong confidant and friend, who continually encouraged me to pursue ministries I might not have considered otherwise.

My first intentional mentoring experience took place while I was president of a Christian college in Nebraska. I was about forty years old, pursuing studies for a Doctor of Ministry degree, and experiencing some stressful days as a college president. One day I went home at lunch time to an empty house, sat down in a chair, and began sobbing uncontrollably. When I shared what happened with my wife, she encouraged me to talk to a psychologist who was teaching a class on our campus.

It did not take long for him to discern that my symptoms were consistent with those of an adult child of an alcoholic (ACA). He was leading a support group of ACAs at the time and encouraged me to join it. Through his intervention, the group's support, and reading more about common social and emotional struggles of ACAs, I was empowered to develop some coping methods to deal with those struggles. I also gained a new appreciation for the need to have mentors help me maneuver through the ebbs and tides of ministry. I was also more open to being a mentor myself, which led to becoming a formal mentor to college and seminary students in ministry studies. I am now "paying it forward"!

THE UNSEEN MENTOR

The real power behind our mentoring relationships is the Unseen Mentor—the Holy Spirit. The development process for pastoral leaders for the twenty-first century will be primarily the work of the Holy Spirit if we remain surrendered to Jesus Christ and open to the Spirit's leading.

It is a tremendous gift to us that God has considered us worthy to be his instruments in the process of mentoring others toward personal and professional maturity. "In the partnership of mentoring, we are helped to pay attention to the movement of the Holy Spirit in the ordinary."[20]

Mentors must first listen to God through the Holy Spirit, then listen to the protégé and respond to his or her needs. Any efforts that rely only on our experience and knowledge will not be sufficient. As we invite the Spirit to lead us, then we will be mentors who are spiritual guides to our protégés.

> Only through such a relationship with the Holy Spirit are we enabled and empowered to participate in the ongoing ministry of Jesus and to discern what the Father wants us

20. Anderson and Reese, *Spiritual Mentoring*, 44.

> to do. Ministry, if it is to be fruitful—not merely productive—must be *through* the Holy Spirit.[21]

As Christian mentors who desire to develop leaders, we must continually seek to live by the Spirit and seek to be filled with the Spirit. As we are Spirit-filled, then we will be mentors who exhibit the fruit of the Spirit with our protégés, and God will be glorified in it all!

ADDITIONAL RESOURCES

Anderson, Keith R., and Randy D. Reese. *Spiritual Mentoring.* Downers Grove, IL: InterVarsity, 1999.

Coleman, Robert E. *The Master Plan of Evangelism.* Grand Rapids, MI: Revell, 1964.

Johnson, W. Brad, and Charles R. Ridley. *The Elements of Mentoring.* New York: Palgrave Macmillan, 2008.

Lewis, Rick. *Mentoring Matters.* Monarch Books, 2009.

Reese, Randy D., and Robert Loane. *Deep Mentoring.* Downers Grove, IL: InterVarsity, 2012.

Smither, Edward L. *Augustine as Mentor: A Model for Preparing Spiritual Leaders.* Nashville, TN: Broadman & Holman Academic, 2008.

Stanley, Paul, and J. Robert Clinton. *Connecting: The Mentoring Relationships You Need to Succeed in Life.* Colorado Springs, CO: NavPress, 1992.

Thomas, Scott, and Tom Wood. *Gospel Coach: Shepherding Leaders to Glorify God.* Grand Rapids, MI: Zondervan, 2012.

Williams, Brian A. *The Potter's Rib: Mentoring for Pastoral Formation.* Vancouver, BC: Regent College Publishing, 2005.

Zachary, Lois J. *The Mentor's Guide.* San Francisco, CA: Jossey-Bass, 2000.

21. Seamands, *Ministry in the Image of God*, 29.

3

PRINCIPLE THREE

Pursue Your Calling Daily

Bill was sitting on the platform in the church building which had been built during his thirty-five-year ministry. As various individuals were sharing their stories about Bill and his ministry with them, he could not help but wonder how he had managed to lead this congregation for so long through many difficult challenges, great victories, and series of young pastors who had served with him through those years.

He came to this congregation as a young pastor with limited experience. He followed a much-loved leader who had helped the congregation experience positive numerical growth and influence in this community of 25,000 people. The elders were experienced men who had worked closely with the former pastor, but had a tendency toward legalism.

In spite of periodical conflicts and confrontations, Bill remained faithful. Even in times of personal crises with his own children, he faithfully led this congregation and its leaders to greater health and effectiveness in ministry. His pastoral skills and his longevity were instrumental in bringing a new spirit into this congregation. It became the most influential congregation in the community, not materially, but spiritually.

So how did Bill manage to serve and lead so faithfully and effectively? He understood that ministry leadership is a "marathon" and not a "sprint." He understood that there will be times of discouragement and difficulty. He understood that faithfulness in leadership requires a daily pursuit. Each new day brings it own possibilities and challenges. And he understood the wonderful, matchless grace of Jesus!

During a period of approximately five years during my preaching ministry, I was seriously involved in running not only for exercise, but also so I could participate in 5K and 10K road races. It was a great time, and my associate minister was my running/training partner. I never was able to beat him in a race, but it was a fun time as we worked out together several mornings a week and traveled together to races. Many of the 5K races included a one-mile "fun run" for children. It was always interesting and humorous to watch these small children take off like bullets when the race started, only to see them a few hundred yards down the road, bending over, trying to catch their breath. To them, the race seemed to be about the beginning. In life and leadership, it is not so much about the beginning as it is the finishing. Many begin well; too few finish well.

The resilient apostle, Paul, understood this principle and even described his life as a "race." Near the end of his life, writing to his young protégé Timothy, he expressed his confidence that he had "finished the race" and was ready to receive the prize which the Lord had for him. This race had not been run with ease, nor with the absence of setbacks. But Paul was convinced of his goal and who would sustain him in the race. He understood that it would take a daily pursuit and require a firm belief that "the steadfast love of the Lord never ceases; his mercies never come to an end; they are *new every morning*; great is your faithfulness." (Lam 3:23).

The resilient pastor will embrace this long-term perspective on personal and leadership development. We do not become mature overnight or without pain. We trust that God is working in us even when it seems that we are in a dry season of our lives. There are several important principles to understand and apply in order to develop this type of perspective in our development.

THE FOUNDATION OF OUR "CALL"

One of the findings from a major study of pastoral leadership in America and Canada was that "the clergy's commitment to their call is strong."[1] In another comment on this topic, Carroll states, "I noted that believing that one is called by God to ordained ministry is an important aspect of a pastor's personal spirituality and provides a kind of moral compass for his or her work in ministry."[2]

But who is ready to accept this high calling? Do not many of us have the urge to flee this calling, as did Gregory of Nazianzus who was later known as one of the three Cappadocian Fathers in the early Church?[3] Or we respond by fleeing, as Jonah did, to our call to proclaim God's message for our generation?

"Calling" can be such a mysterious and confusing word. My experience with many students is that they really do not have much clarity about the concept or that their understanding of the term is highly conditioned by their prior experiences in dysfunctional churches and/or negative cultural images. If Carroll and others are correct in their emphasis, then it is important to gain a clearer understanding of "calling."

An examination of biblical leaders reveals a diversity of the ways in which they came to their leadership roles. Some received a dramatic call from God (e.g., Moses, Samuel, Paul), others were appointed by existing leaders (e.g., Joshua, Titus), and others rose to leadership as their gifts were recognized (e.g., Joseph, Barnabas,

1. Carroll, *God's Potters*, 162. This book is the compilation of the findings from this major study funded by the Lilly Endowment. It is self-described as "the most representative survey of Protestant and Catholic clergy ever undertaken."

2. Ibid.

3. See Williams, *The Potter's Rib*, 13–41, for a detailed account of Gregory's struggle with his call to ministry.

Timothy). "Throughout history God has provided societies with leaders, even if they have fulfilled their calling in different ways and through various forms and structures of authority."[4]

There is a sense of *general calling* in every believer's life. It is the call to be a Christ-follower. It is a call to surrender in obedience to the Lord Jesus Christ. It is a call to live a life worthy of the Lord Jesus (Eph 4:1). It is a call to be a minister/servant in the place where God has called, whether as a factory worker, lawyer, nurse, homemaker, or politician.

The sense of being called to spiritual leadership is a different sense of calling. For some, this sense of calling is dramatic. For others, this call is more a process. It involves a recognition that God has a specific intention for one's life.

> It involves personal awareness of a special call to God's service. The ministry activity and leadership agendas that flow from it focus on the spiritual development of others. Spiritual leaders help others live out their callings in their families, their personal mission expressions, their church life.[5]

God has provided leaders for his people throughout history. In the Old Testament we observe prophets, priests, wise men, and elders who served as leaders. In the New Testament we find apostles, prophets, evangelists, and pastors/teachers (Eph 4:11). God has gifted and equipped various leaders who can lead others at the appropriate time and location.

The need for the church today is leaders who are called, gifted, and equipped for leadership roles. As many writers have noted, the calling may be private, but it is confirmed publicly by other mature Christians. Each potential leader must ask, "Do my gifts, abilities, and passion appear to line up with my sense of calling?" This question is best answered collectively with other believers, not individually.

4. Tidball, *Ministry by the Book*, 13.

5. McNeal, *A Work of Heart*, 98.

Once an individual has determined that this is a sincere, God-directed, church-confirmed calling, then a process begins of discovering to what particular areas of ministry leadership God is calling. This may even change during the course of one's life.

Resiliency in ministry is supported by a deep conviction that this is the work to which God has called us. When we "hit the wall" in leadership, our sense of calling will strengthen our resolve to remain faithful.

SPIRITUAL WARFARE

To accept the mantle of pastoral leadership is to live dangerously! Every individual who accepts Jesus as Lord enters into an intense spiritual battle, but pastoral ministry especially places one in a hazardous position. Our spiritual enemy will use every tool at his disposal to damage us, discourage us, and defeat us.

The enemy is so bold in his attacks that he even sought to tempt Jesus to turn away from God's call in his life. In Luke 4, we read about the enemy's confrontation with Jesus, as our Lord himself faced a decision whether or not he would enter into his ministry or turn aside from that ministry and accept a different role in his life. And this confrontation followed immediately upon that mountaintop experience of his baptism and the Father's declaration of his favor!

If Jesus faced such a challenge from the enemy, why would we not assume that the enemy will seek to attack us and destroy us and the witness of the Church? Luke's gospel reveals that Jesus steadfastly pursued his ministry and refused to be turned aside from the Father's purpose. It also reveals that one of the key factors in his success was his intimacy with God. Two early examples of this are found in Luke 4:42 and 5:16.

Paul warned Timothy that in "later times some will depart from the faith by devoting themselves to deceitful spirits and teachings of demons" (1 Tim 4:1). With this challenge and with the teaching which Paul had given earlier to the churches about spiritual warfare (Eph 6:10–18), Timothy would not be ignorant about the cosmic battle that he was engaging in as a leader in the church of Jesus Christ.

Unfortunately, many Christian leaders today seem to give little credence to this matter of spiritual warfare. But the biblical record in both the Old and New Testaments is very clear about the existence of demonic powers which seek to destroy believers.

> The Scriptures abound with military images of conflict, warfare, and adversaries in the believer's life. It is not a question of whether we are engaged in a spiritual warfare; the question is how effectively we are fighting. . . . For us to be overcomers, we need discipline, resistance, the skillful use of spiritual weapons, and dependence upon the power of God.[6]

I do not pretend to understand everything about spiritual warfare. I do know that our enemy loves to destroy us and to destroy the testimony of the Church. He will work in subtle and in blatant ways. We must be aware of both.

There are two vital resources that are available to Christians in fighting this spiritual battle. First, there is the confidence we gain from knowing that Jesus Christ himself has prayed for us: "I do not ask that you take them out of the world, but that you keep them from the evil one" (John 17:15). Also, we know that Jesus continues to intercede for us (Rom 8:34).

Second, we have the resource of intercessory prayer. Paul understood the power of prayer for one another as we face this battle. As he closed the section of his letter to the Ephesian churches about spiritual warfare, he exhorted the believers to "pray in the Spirit at all times." And in 2 Thessalonians, we read his exhortation about intercessory prayer for himself and for others:

> Finally, brothers, pray for us, that the word of the Lord may speed ahead and be honored, as happened among you, and that we may be delivered from wicked and evil men. For not all have faith. But the Lord is faithful. He will establish you and guard you against the evil one.[7]

6. Boa, *Conformed to His Image*, 19.

7. 2 Thess 3:1–3.

I am also encouraged by the words of Trevor Hudson concerning intercessory prayer:

> There is a cosmic struggle taking place, and every time we intercede we increase the openings through which God's power can freely flow. Resurrection faith believes that, while destructive spiritual forces can impede God's purposes, our intercessions for the coming of the kingdom will ultimately prevail. The empty tomb reminds us that no matter how entrenched and pervasive these powers, the victory shall be with God.[8]

The resilient pastor affirms that we are in a spiritual battle and that there are times when that battle is very intense. Our enemy will attack us from within and from outside. But we can rise above our fear with confidence that Jesus is praying for us and that we have fellow believers who are bringing us to God's throne as well. The latter assumes that we are in relationship with others who know us, love us, and want the best for us.

NEHEMIAH: FAITHFUL IN ADVERSITY

At different times in holy history, God selected an individual and entrusted him or her with a major task for his people. In 445 BC, God selected Nehemiah to go to Jerusalem to lead the rebuilding of the walls. In the midst of consistent opposition, Nehemiah remained faithful to his call and *pursued daily* his God and his mission.

Nehemiah was a leader who understood the importance of prayer and worship. Upon learning the condition of the exiles in Jerusalem, Nehemiah wept for days. He also fasted, repented, and prayed. Indeed, he persisted in prayer for four months before he approached King Artaxerxes with his request to go to Jerusalem. His concern was not for himself, but for God's honor and glory.

8. Hudson, *Discovering our Spiritual Identity*, 123.

He met opposition immediately upon his arrival in Jerusalem. His natural reaction to the opposition was prayer and spending time listening to God. He then proceeded to evaluate the situation and began to build his team to meet the challenge.

Reading through the book of Nehemiah, it is clear that Satan wanted to destroy Nehemiah and his mission. There was opposition all around him, and the enemy was using tools of intimidation and threats. But Nehemiah remained true to his calling and leaned upon the Lord for strength and courage.

In an amazing feat, the ruined walls of Jerusalem were rebuilt in fifty-two days! Revival occurred in Israel, and God was glorified. The prescribed means of worshipping God could be renewed.

God called Nehemiah to a difficult task. Nehemiah responded to God's call, humbled himself, and leaned upon God's strength. He faced challenges from his enemies and the challenge of directing a building project that would require great wisdom and much administrative responsibility. Through it all, Nehemiah kept close to God and persevered to the completion of the goal, knowing that there would be new challenges facing him after that.

LEADERSHIP STRESSORS

Stress is a given in life and leadership. The level of stress may ebb and flow depending on the season of life, organizational context, external circumstances, and relational demands. But it is an ever-present reality. While most of my mentoring work is done with pastors and seminarians, I have two sons who are both involved in high-pressure, stressful work environments. While there are unique variations to a pastor's work, many young leaders also face tremendous challenges in their contexts.

Unique Challenges for Pastoral Leaders

Work of ministry is never done: There will always be one more sermon to preach, one more lesson to teach, one more person to comfort, one more crisis to confront.

- Results of ministry are difficult to measure: There are some quantitative aspects which can be measured for ministry effectiveness, but primarily, the results will not be known for years.
- Leading a primarily volunteer-led organization has challenges: It is difficult to confront or "fire" volunteers.
- The nature of pastoral work requires much time with very "needy" people: This is the type of ministry Christ calls us to, but it is draining.
- Many functions of ministry require the pastor to operate out of his or her "persona": This is especially true of many key life events, such as weddings and funerals.
- Lack of clarity and unity concerning the mission and goals of the church: This is often driven by the perceptions of what is happening in large, popular ministries rather than a local context evaluation and determination.

H. B. London and Neil B. Wiseman provide a list of twenty "hazards of ministry" which also provide some good insights into the unique challenges for pastoral leaders.[9]

The Stress of Leading for Change

The nature of gospel ministry is leading others toward change. It is helping others to change individually (think repentance and sanctification), and it is helping congregations to change collectively (think mission and worship).

Since change is at the heart of pastoral leadership, it guarantees that the leader will face conflict. This is true because of the

9. London and Wiseman, *Pastors at Greater Risk*, 35–59.

axiom articulated well by Ronald Heifitz and Marty Linsky: "If leadership were about giving people good news, the job would be easy . . . people do not resist change, per se. People resist loss."[10] Heifetz and Linsky continue by observing that "Leadership becomes dangerous, then, when it must confront people with loss."[11]

Resilient pastoral leaders understand these principles and dynamics. While most of us take no joy in dealing with conflict, we must accept the fact that it is a natural part of ministry leadership because we are calling individuals and groups to change. We must not be naïve and think that any of us can avoid all conflict. In fact, Fuller Theological Seminary has reported that 40 percent of pastors have reported a serious conflict with a parishioner at least once a month.[12] Long-term conflict will bring great stress and can be accompanied by physiological symptoms.

THREE IMPORTANT TOOLS FOR LEADING THROUGH TIMES OF CHANGE

The reality of leading through change necessitates that pastoral leaders be equipped with tools in order to more effectively manage the process personally and corporately.

Tool # 1: Understanding the Dynamics of Grief

If change involves a sense of loss, then that sense of loss will result in an experience of grief. Indeed, grief is the one of the most universal dynamics that we face as people and as leaders. Therefore, if we are to lead well and to guide others through this process, it is important to understand the typical dynamics of grief.

There are various presentations about the dynamics of grief and the stages of loss. One of the most helpful for pastoral leaders

10. Heifetz and Linsky, *Leadership on the Line*, 11.

11. Ibid., 13.

12. Fuller Institute, *1991 Survey of Pastors.*

is that of Granger Westberg in his book, *Good Grief*. Below are the ten stages of grief as expressed by Westberg:

1. We are in a state of shock.
2. We express emotion.
3. We feel depressed and lonely.
4. We may experience physical symptoms of distress.
5. We may become panicky.
6. We feel a sense of guilt about the loss.
7. We are filled with hostility and resentment.
8. We are unable to return to usual activities.
9. Gradually hope comes through.
10. We struggle to affirm reality.[13]

There will be many factors involved which help determine the strength and depth of these reactions, but the leader must be aware of them and seek to maintain a healthy, non-reactive presence in the midst of them.

Tool # 2: Common Reactions to Change

As it is important to remember the stages of grief that individuals may experience as the result of losses, it is also valuable to have a perspective on the common reactions that people have to change. I have found the material by Ken Blanchard and Phil Hodges in *The Servant Leader* to provide a good framework for considering these reactions:

1. People will feel awkward, ill at ease, and self-conscious when confronted by change.
2. People will feel alone even if everyone else is going through the same change.

13. Westberg, *Good Grief*.

3. People will think first about what they have to give up.
4. People will think they can only handle so much change at once.
5. People will be concerned that they don't have enough resources (time, money, skills, etc.) to implement the change.
6. People will be at different levels of readiness for any particular change.
7. If pressure is taken off, people will revert to old behaviors.[14]

The authors provide suggestions for leaders on how to handle these reactions in order to lead people and the organization effectively.

Tool # 3: Strategies on Dealing with Conflict

The third tool is a list of eight strategies for dealing with conflict which is found in Reggie McNeal's *A Work of Heart*. Those strategies will be listed below with a quote or two under each one:

Strategy One: Get Over It

"If you want to emerge better through conflict, go ahead and die. Die to expectations that everyone will love you."

Strategy Two: Choose Your Pain

"The leader who is going nowhere will take hits from all sides. The leader who sets a direction will at least know what direction the arrows will be coming from."

Strategy Three: Examine Your Critics

"When criticism comes, the smart leader knows how to weigh it."

14. Blanchard and Hodges, *The Servant Leader*, 66–67.

> "Effective spiritual leaders understand that the presenting issue is not always the real issue . . . perhaps (and often) the struggle is over control."

Strategy Four: Look in the Mirror

"While examining critics or opponents, the leader must also initiate a thorough self-examination."

Strategy Five: Get Good Advice

"Counselors are especially helpful during conflict."

> "Cultivating godly people as confidants and advisers helps a leader prepare to endure hardships."

Strategy Six: Be Kind and Honest

"The leader can always afford to be kind, and must deal in honesty. Both elements are essential to the leader's emerging from conflict strengthened in the heart by the experience."

Strategy Seven: Forgive!

"The power to forgive is a Godlike quality that blesses others by releasing them from the power of a poor past."

Strategy Eight: Make a Decision

"The leader who grows through leadership challenges has not done so accidentally. This leader has made a decision to grow."[15]

15. McNeal, *A Work of Heart*, Chapter 9.

TIM MCCOY: LEADING THROUGH CHANGE

When my wife, Beverly, and I arrived in Macon, Georgia, to begin our first full-time, post-seminary ministry, I don't think anyone really imagined that we would still be serving this *same* church twenty-five years later. We certainly did not.

And the truth is that Ingleside Baptist Church really is *not* the same church today as it was a quarter century ago. By God's grace, it's been a remarkable journey of growth and change.

How significant has the change been? Let me illustrate with a few key metrics and observations. We have journeyed from about 500 worshipers then to more than 2,000 now; from a budget of $800,000 then to almost $6,000,000 now; from a campus of 9 acres then to more than 22 acres now.

The journey has led us from music that was more traditional . . . to blended . . . to contemporary . . . and now all three styles in four services each weekend; from typical Baptist governance to a simpler structure. The list could go on.

As I have led through these changes, I have learned a few lessons related to vision, values, time, trust, partners, faith, and the cost of *leading through change*.

Vision—All these changes at Ingleside have been driven by a vision of glorifying God by making disciples of Jesus Christ. Constancy and clarity of purpose actually enables change.

Values—When a specific change has been clearly connected to an unchanging, cherished, and biblical value, our church has embraced the new initiatives more eagerly.

Time—While less can be accomplished in a year than you probably think, more can be accomplished in five or ten years than you likely imagine. Change implemented incrementally has preserved unity and conserved gains. Take the longer view.

Trust—Leading change is easier where trust abounds. Trust grows as I am Christ-like in my character, consistent, and compassionate. Regularly "asking for forgiveness rather than permission" diminishes trust. Play by the rules until you lead the rules to be changed.

Partners—Significant change is never implemented alone. Apart from a sizable cast of "partners in the gospel" (Phil 1:5), the changes at Ingleside could not have occurred.

Faith—Leading change means a willingness to believe that God can and will do "immeasurably more than all we ask or imagine" (Eph 3:20, NIV). Nurture your faith in God's Word daily.

Cost—The price is high to lead effectively through change. Most change in our church has required me to change first. Count the cost. Trust that God's grace will be sufficient. Then, lead change. It will be worth it.

Twenty-five years into this journey of leading change at Ingleside, I have a heart filled with gratitude and continue to be convinced that *the best is yet to come!*

PSEUDO ANSWERS TO MAINTAINING A DAILY PURSUIT

When a leader does not take the longer view of personal leadership development, it is easy to fall prey to thoughts and actions that sabotage one's progress. Many leaders under stress or dealing with difficult circumstances will resort to what I term as "pseudo answers" to the situation. There are four common ones that I observe:

1. *Work harder and work more hours*—it is believed that if one can somehow give more time and greater effort then one will succeed. This answer is even reinforced by some well-meaning Christians who are in supervisory roles with these leaders. This response fails to take a holistic view of an individual's current work and life context.
2. *Change the scene*—What this usually means is to relocate. Find a different employment position. It may address some

connections had resulted in several requests for Barbara to join various community organizations and serve on boards. She also was invited to speak for some community functions.

In the middle of her second year of ministry, after a particularly hectic week, Barbara realized that her preparation time for her sermons had dwindled to less than three hours per week and that she was relying more and more on sermon books from denominational preachers. Her greatest love and strength had become something to fit into her schedule on Friday or Saturday. She realized she needed help.

Barbara had become an example of someone who had settled for the "good" and was neglecting the "best." Her ministry had all the signs of being effective and fruitful, but she knew that her personal priorities were in need of rearrangement. In the terms of this chapter, Barbara was failing to focus on the core values which were a part of her being. She had not been mentored concerning this area of her life, nor had she invested the time to write out her vision and priorities. It was an exercise that would have great value for her. In the words of Stephen Covey, Barbara was not "putting first things first." She was allowing the "urgent, but not important" issues to crowd out the "not urgent, but important" issues in her life.[1]

JESUS: FOCUSED LEADER

Early in his public ministry, Jesus made it very clear that the Father's purpose for him was the purpose to which he would give his energy and time. Luke records Jesus' inaugural sermon in Nazareth in which he quotes from Isaiah 61 to indicate his mission and purpose. Utilizing the text in Luke, Jesus states:

> The Spirit of the Lord is upon me, because he has anointed me to proclaim good news to the poor. He has sent me to proclaim liberty to the captives and recovering of sight

1. Covey, *The 7 Habits*, 145–182.

> to the blind, to set at liberty those who are oppressed, to proclaim the year of the Lord's favor.[2]

Later in this same chapter in Luke, Jesus resists the crowds who would want to set his agenda. He tells them, "I must preach the good news of the kingdom of God to the other towns as well; for I was sent for this purpose."[3] Even Peter, one of the apostles in Jesus' inner circle, had to be confronted when he sought to derail Jesus from his ultimate purpose. Jesus remained committed and focused.

While remaining focused on his purpose, Jesus did not ignore or neglect the ministry needs around him. He still touched the sick, the tired, and the discouraged. But he never lost sight of his mission to proclaim the kingdom of God in all its fullness and to embody the message of salvation which would be provided through his own death.

PERSONAL CORE VALUES

Your core values reflect your heart and soul. They are the internal standards by which you choose to live your life. They should guide what you think, how you feel, how you make decisions, and how you act. Your values are shaped by your beliefs and developed by study, reflection, and interaction with others. For the Christian leader, the primary value-shaping factors should be the Word of God and the Holy Spirit.

I have said for many years that there are two items which, when observed, will reveal an individual's values: the calendar and the checkbook. Our regular behaviors show what we really value. So, here is how one begins to formalize and embrace his values.

First, examine the past two weeks of your life. Actually list the number of hours given to your various activities (e.g., sleep, watching TV, internet/Facebook time, work, etc.). This will reveal what you actually value through the allotment of your time.

2. Luke 4:18–19.

3. Luke 4:43.

Second, examine your personal and family expenditures for the past month. This will reveal what you actually value through the allotment of your finances. Here is how you might chart this exercise in a notebook or on your electronic device:

Activity/Expenditures	Value

After completing this honest "audit" of your time and finances, you can see if your life is really revealing the values which you claim to hold. One example of inconsistency that I observe with most Christians is that we claim to value the Great Commission and evangelism in general, but have not shared our faith with an unbeliever for months!

Now, you are ready to make a formal list of your core values. Try to keep your list to ten items or less. After you have compiled this list, then complete the chart below:

Because I believe . . .	I value . . .	Therefore, I commit to . . .

The convictions that result from this exercise will need time to implement. Also, if one is married, it will be crucial to process this together with your spouse. Now, you are ready to proceed to the development of your personal vision/mission statement.

PERSONAL VISION/MISSION STATEMENT

The development of a personal vision/mission statement can be a helpful exercise that will provide a written reminder of one's ultimate goal and purpose. As a Christian leader, this will help you to remain focused as you are tempted to dilute your time and energy with activities that are "good," but not centered in your core mission.

There are two quotes which accentuate the value of a written statement which I find helpful in my own leadership journey:

> It is easy to say "no!" when there's a deeper "yes" inside . . . vision is that deeper "yes!" burning inside. —Covey and Merrill
>
> Your "no's" give value to your "yes's." —Arch Hart

In the case study in the beginning of this chapter, this was Barbara's problem. She was saying "yes" too often and "no" too infrequently.

One simple illustration of the need to practice these principles is the number of invitations you will receive to participate in various boards or activities in local organizations as you become more integrated into the community where you serve. As the pastor of a growing, thriving congregation, I established a policy that I would not serve on the board of more than one organization at a time. This included our regional Christian college board. This practice may result in some hurt feelings or misunderstandings but will help protect you from burnout or "vision slip."

A personal vision/mission statement needs to come from the core of who you are in Christ and how he has gifted you for ministry. It will flow from your sense of purpose and your passions. It will provide the focus, energy, and direction for your decisions and your actions.

My simple personal vision/mission statement for my ministry is:

> I will use my gifts and energy to recruit, teach, mentor, and encourage students who desire to grow in Christ and desire to serve him through serving his Church.

Obviously, this is contextualized to my current ministry. When I was in local parish ministry, it reflected that context.

Here is a simple process for developing one's own personal vision/mission statement:

Step One: Reflect on Jesus and his grace in your salvation and your calling.

Step Two: Examine your passions—what fills you, what energizes you.

Step Three: Examine your gifts, skills, and training.

Step Four: Reflect on the Great Commandment and the Great Commission.

Step Five: Write your first draft of your statement.

Step Six: Review your statement with your mentor (and your spouse, if married).

Step Seven: Rewrite your statement, and review it at least weekly.

Once you have completed your core values chart and your personal vision/mission statement, you are ready to develop a personal philosophy of ministry. These three items together will assist you in focusing on core values, especially in times of adversity.

TITUS: "PUT INTO ORDER"

Titus was another of Paul's closest protégés. He was a Gentile believer (Gal 2:3) who accompanied Paul and Barnabas to Jerusalem (Gal 2:1) to speak to the apostles about their mission. The relationship of this young leader to Paul is described by Paul in endearing terms, as Paul called him "my true child in common faith."[4]

4. Titus 1:4.

Paul had entrusted Titus with two difficult tasks to the church in Corinth. Titus delivered Paul's difficult letter to the Corinthians, and he was entrusted with the collection of the money for the needy Christians. Titus later accompanied Paul to Crete where Paul left him with the task of leading the church there. Given the culture of Crete, this would have been a very challenging task.

Not only had Paul mentored Titus, but he must have held great confidence in him to leave him in Crete to face such a daunting task. Paul had invested in his spiritual development and his leadership skills. Now, Titus was given the responsibility to live up to *his core values and to fulfill the mission* which he had been given.

Paul's personal appointment of Titus would have provided some sense of authority for him to begin within this ministry. After Paul's departure, Titus is to "put what remained into order and appoint elders."[5] The lack of mature Christians in Crete would have presented a challenge for Titus to fulfill this charge, and false teaching had already become a challenge as well.

Paul's letter to Titus is filled with exhortations for him to live a godly life and to lead with integrity and wisdom. He is to lead out of a strong conviction of what he knows and believes. He is to remain focused on his mission of equipping and leading the church in Crete to a place of being a faithful, godly witness to their corrupt culture.

PERSONAL PHILOSOPHY OF MINISTRY

A personal philosophy of ministry statement includes a set of biblical values that inform ministry, the leader's own giftedness, and personal leadership core values. One's philosophy of ministry guides ministry decisions and staffing decisions, and it serves as a means for evaluating the practice of ministry in one's context.

5. Titus 1:5.

The philosophy of ministry statement should:

- Be faithful to Scripture (but it is *not* a doctrinal statement)
- Reflect one's own giftedness and personal strengths
- Be sensitive to the current culture and one's anticipated ministry context

Appendix Two provides two examples of philosophy of ministry statements. This statement may be used as an important tool to assist church leaders who are considering an individual for a ministry position.

SUMMARY

When we are beginning a journey, it is important to have our destination in mind. It is also important to have the tools we need to assist us along the way, especially when we face challenges and adversity. Written statements of our core values, our personal vision/mission, and our philosophy of ministry will serve as guides when the way becomes dark or clouded. When others would seek to distract us or lead us away from the purpose our God has for us, we can meet the challenge with strength as we are reminded of the basics.

CHUCK SACKETT: FOCUSED LEADER

I had no intention of being in ministry. I went to a Christian college simply because I was so biblically ignorant. While I was there, God tricked me (that's how it felt) into being a preacher.

I soon discovered what many discovered: Ministry is messy. At first I survived because of my wife and a good friend. Then, I learned to lean on my sense of calling. If this was God's idea, then he would have to supply the strength to get it done, and he did.

Writing out my calling has been one of the most helpful activities I've performed. I revisit my calling regularly to remind me that this is God's business, not mine. At least annually, I also revisit the call statements of two other preachers: one, Jeremiah 1:4–10; the other in James Earl Massey's book, *The Burdensome Joy of Preaching*.

A few years into ministry I discovered the power of a personal mission and values statement. I framed a statement that captured what I believed I was gifted for and the values that I believed were most important to my calling.

I've not only learned that ministry is messy, I've also learned that ministry is seductive. There is so much opportunity and so many needs. As the opportunities arise to get more involved, I find myself returning to my mission statement. Does this activity fit? Does it interfere with other ministry opportunities I'm committed to? Can I give the time these commitments deserve? If not, I have no business saying "yes."

I keep a "Mag Light" at my house. It has an adjustable beam that can produce a flood of light or a tightly focused beam. It does an adequate job as a flood light, but its focused beam is much more helpful. My calling and my core values/ mission keep me focused.

I value the preaching of the Word of God, the role of local congregations in facilitating life transformation, and character above even competence and chemistry. Therefore, everything I choose to do must develop godly leaders for churches committed to seeing lives changed through the preaching and teaching of the Gospel.

At the most practical level, I limit my involvement in community and ecclesial affairs to only those that advance the gospel of Christ through the local church's proclamation of Jesus. Then, when invitations arise, I have a basis for my decisions. I simply review my core values and my personal calling and decide if the invitation fits.

ADDITIONAL RESOURCES

Blanchard, Ken, and Phil Hodges. *The Servant Leader.* Nashville, TN: Countryman, 2003.

Covey, Stephen R. *The 7 Habits of Highly Effective People.* New York: Fireside, 1989.

Figliuolo, Mike. *One Piece of Paper.* San Francisco, CA: Jossey-Bass, 2011.

George, Bill. *True North.* San Francisco, CA: Jossey-Bass, 2007

Perman, Matt. *What's Best Next.* Grand Rapids, MI: Zondervan, 2014.

5

PRINCIPLE FIVE

Recognize Your Strengths

Steve was a promising new graduate of one of the prominent seminaries in his denomination. He had received much recognition from fellow students and faculty members as a leader among the student body. His wife had been fully supportive of Steve's seminary work and she worked two part-time jobs to assure that Steve would not have to work while he completed his degree.

Upon graduation, Steve found it more difficult than he had imagined to find a ministry position. He felt called to minister in a local church context through using his gifts of teaching and preaching. His desire was to serve as the solo pastor of a small church or as senior pastor of a medium-size congregation. He soon became frustrated in his search for a ministry position as he was only receiving interest from churches that were looking for a student ministry pastor.

Finally, Steve reluctantly accepted the call to serve as pastor to students, junior high and senior high youth, at a church in a nearby state. He and his wife wanted to start a family, so they wanted her to be able to stop working, or at least take a several months leave from a job.

It became evident quickly that the expectations of the

congregational leaders and the parents of the youth were that Steve would function as a "recreation and entertainment director." There was little interest from the youth or their parents in biblical instruction or intentional discipleship.

After eighteen months, Steve and his wife were discouraged, even depressed. His conversations with his senior pastor and the leaders provided no relief or direction. Feeling totally defeated and discouraged, Steve resigned, and they moved back to their home town. He found a job in a bank operated by a family friend and had no interest in seeking another ministry position.

Unfortunately, I have witnessed Steve's story being repeated multiple times in my own career of seminary teaching as new graduates accept ministries which do not fit their gifts or strengths. Out of desperation, many students have accepted a ministry which they knew would most likely lead to frustration. In Steve's case, there were many factors which were out of his control. But there were also some that should have served as major warning signs for him *before* he accepted this position.

Even though his statement will need some clarification and qualification, Aubrey Malphurs expresses an important ministry leadership principle in his book, *Maximizing Your Effectiveness*. "I am convinced that believers will not experience the joy and satisfaction of authentic ministry until they are serving Christ in ministries consistent with how God designed them: with their spiritual gifts, passions, temperaments, talents, abilities, and leadership styles."[1]

I believe that when we understand and recognize how God has shaped us personally for ministry and leadership roles, then we will be able to become proactive in our search for those roles. This understanding includes these items listed by Malphurs—our spiritual gifts, passions, abilities, talents, and temperaments.

1. Malphurs, *Maximizing Your Effectiveness*, 11.

However, I also understand that it is a rare occurrence that a ministry leader can serve *only* in areas of strength. Most of us will be called to serve in roles that involve areas outside of our strengths as well as those in our strengths. The important factor to consider is that if we are not serving in our areas of strength, giftedness, and passion at least 60–70 percent of the time, we will be more prone to discouragement, frustration, and burnout.

The mistake many church leaders (lay and clergy) make is to assume that an individual can be coached into someone they are not, with strengths they do not possess. While it is possible to make minor changes in one's style, it is impossible to transform completely these basic personal issues. God has shaped us and equipped us according to His plan, using various circumstances of life. He wants us to serve out of our strengths and giftedness.

PAUL'S TEACHING ON "BODY LIFE"

There are three important passages of Scripture in which the apostle Paul focuses on how the Spirit gifts and shapes us for ministry: Romans 12, 1 Corinthians 12, and Ephesians 4. Three important truths which can be gleaned from these passages are:

1. All believers have been given a spiritual gift (or gifts) by the Holy Spirit.
2. God distributes the spiritual gifts according to *his* plan, not because we seek for them.
3. Each believer has a contribution to make to the body of Christ, and therefore is to be a steward of his or her gifts.

While these truths apply to every Christian, it is especially important for each leader to embrace them personally and for his or her leadership philosophy. No leader has all the gifts required for maintaining the health and growth of the church, and that must be acknowledged and accepted. No leader should dismiss the gifts of others but rather seek to provide opportunities for them to utilize those gifts.

There are two other important principles from Paul's teaching which I believe need to be addressed by each leader. First, the leadership gifts are given *to serve* and *to equip*. They are not given to provide support for the leader's authority and control in the body. Second, utilizing your gifts is not for the purpose of bringing attention to your abilities but to nurture and empower others to be released for greater ministry. Peter's teaching on gifts reminds us of the ultimate purpose for using our gifts: "in order that in everything God may be glorified through Jesus Christ" (1 Pet 4:11).

DISCOVERING OUR SPIRITUAL GIFTS

Discovering one's spiritual gifts is part of the process of recognizing one's strengths. As stated above, ministry will be more fruitful and fulfilling when one functions primarily out of areas of strength, giftedness, and passion.

What is a spiritual gift? The place to begin in understanding spiritual gifts is with Paul's teaching in the passages noted above. A simple definition of a spiritual gift is "a unique , God-given ability for service."[2] They are given to the various members of the church in order to fulfill various ministry functions within the body.

There are many books and other materials available to assist a believer to help discover one's spiritual gifts. Spiritual gifts inventories can be helpful instruments for this process, even though there is a high level of subjectivity involved. The "Gifted2Serve"[3] online spiritual gifts inventory is recommended for current leaders to use in this process; this inventory is available at www.buildingchurch.net/g2s. Other resources are listed in the "Additional Resources" at the end of this chapter.

Most pastoral leaders will have more than one gift. The combination of these gifts is known as your *gift-mix*. For example,

2. Malphurs, *Maximizing Your Effectiveness*, 46.

3. Kulp, *Gifted2Serve*.

shepherd may be one's top gift, but the gifts of leadership, teaching, and wisdom are also rated highly. The combination would be this individual's *gift-mix.*

Don Cousins makes some key observations concerning leaders and giftedness in his book, *Experiencing LeaderShift*. Cousins believes that many current leaders in churches have become discouraged in their roles because they do not have the spiritual gift of leadership. They have the role of "leader" and therefore believe they must have this gift. Cousins argues, and I believe rightfully so, that pastors lead in many different ways through the use of their specific gifts and abilities. They do not have to have the spiritual gift of "leadership" in order to influence the growth and health of their particular context. Cousins provides five examples of how this occurs through various gifts that have a leadership effect.

1. The apostle *leads* through the launching of a new work.
2. The prophet *leads* by bringing a message that edifies and exhorts.
3. The evangelist *leads* by proclaiming the gospel to those who aren't yet saved.
4. The pastor *leads* by shepherding a group of people.
5. The teacher *leads* by providing instruction from the Word.[4]

So, we take a spiritual gifts inventory to assist us in recognizing our strengths. The results of the inventory must be kept in proper perspective as we consider our total divine shaping and our passions. Our role as a leader is not to be defined simply by the use of one instrument or one area of pastoral formation.

Another important component in this process is to seek the counsel of others who have the privilege of observing your ministry. They can help you affirm or revise your understanding of your giftedness.

4. Cousins, *Experiencing LeaderShift*, 35.

BARNABAS AND PAUL: DIFFERING GIFTS

The great missionary apostle of the New Testament church had a less than enthusiastic reception from his fellow believers after his dramatic conversion experience on the road to Damascus. After escaping a plot by the Jews to kill him, Paul went to Jerusalem to join his brothers and sisters there. They were afraid of him. He needed a mentor who was known and respected by the believers in Jerusalem. Barnabas was that mentor for him.

Barnabas believed in Paul and took a risk by commending him to the apostles. Apparently, Barnabas had a conviction that this man was going to be used by God in a great way in the establishment of the church. Later, after the leaders of the church in Jerusalem had sent Barnabas to Antioch to encourage the believers there, Barnabas found Paul and brought him to Antioch so they could teach together and build up the disciples (Acts 11:25–26). In a short time, Paul became the primary leader among the two. Barnabas had encouraged Paul, taken a risk by endorsing him, provided opportunities for Paul to use his gifts, and recognized that his protégé had grown beyond his influence.

Both Barnabas and Paul were recognized leaders in the church. Their contributions were different, but both important. Both were teachers. Barnabas had the gift of encouragement. Paul had the gift of an apostle (missionary/church planter). Both *recognized their strengths*.

The two men had different personalities as well. Paul was strong-willed and direct. Barnabas was more sensitive and gracious. These differences surely played a part in their sharp disagreement over including Mark in the second missionary journey. However, it did not destroy their respect for one another's ministries (cf. 1 Cor 9:6).

Paul's teaching about the "body of Christ" in 1 Corinthians 12 provides a strong example of the necessity of differing gifts and personalities in the church. Without these differences, many needs within the body would go unmet. Without these differences, many opportunities for witness would go unfulfilled.

PERSONALITY STYLE AND LEADERSHIP

A second area of exploration in discovering our strengths is our personality style and the implications of that style. Our personalities are more the "nature" part of our being rather than the "nurture" part which has been involved in the shaping of who we are.

Our personality style is our essential nature. It is how we relate to the world around us. It is God-given and is uniquely ours. Various instruments have been utilized to help individuals gain a better understanding of their personality styles (or "types"). Two popular instruments are the DiSC Classic and the Myers-Briggs Type Indicator. Inscape Publishing provides a comparison of these two instruments.[5]

"*DiSC Classic* is primarily suited for increasing self-awareness in a setting where the individual can decide how to use the information in his or her relations with others."[6] The convenience, reliability, and applicability of the DiSC make it the instrument which I recommend for emerging leaders. It provides an easily understood framework for discussing personality style and its impact upon relationships—personal and professional. It is available in many different formats.

A brief overview of the characteristics of the four styles is provided in Appendix Three. After completing the inventory, it is important to find one's "blended profile" in order to consider various applications. Various sources for these profiles are available online. As noted above, there are helpful applications for personal and professional contexts. This inventory is a common instrument

5. Inscape, *A Comparison*.

6. Ibid., 4.

used by consultants who assist organizations in building team dynamics.[7]

MAXIMIZE STRENGTHS, COMPENSATE FOR WEAKNESSES

One of the biggest mistakes made by many leaders who serve in supervisory roles is to believe that an individual should spend the greatest amount of time on trying to develop more proficiency in his or her greatest areas of weakness. This usually results in more frustration and less success for the individual and the organization.

This dynamic underscores the importance of knowing the strengths and weaknesses of each member of the leadership team. The time dedicated to this process will serve great benefits to each member and for the overall fruitfulness of the group.

Buckingham and Clifton have provided a helpful resource for looking at the unique talents possessed by an individual and how to develop those talents. Their book, *Now, Discover Your Strengths,* is one way to invest in this process. They make the following statement in the introduction to their book:

> These are the two assumptions that guide the world's best managers:
>
> 1. Each person's talents are enduring and unique.
> 2. Each person's greatest room for growth is in the areas of his or her greatest strength.[8]

While this is true, it is important to remember that it is possible for one's greatest strength to become a weakness when it is overdone, especially if the needs of other people are ignored or unappreciated.

7. Another good resource for ministry leaders is the "Solving the People Puzzle" Seminar by Walk Thru the Bible Ministries. This seminar uses the DiSC concepts to help Christians understand themselves, how to celebrate the differences of one another, and how to motivate others for ministry. See www.walkthru.org.

8. Buckingham and Clifton, *Now, Discover Your Strengths*, 8.

CHRIS WINFORD: UNDERSTANDING AND USING ONE'S STRENGTHS

I began my pastoral life full of passion to change the world for Christ. However, all too quickly I was disillusioned into discovering that other people stood in my way. Alarmingly, it was those in church leadership positions who did not think, lead, or respond to situations as I did with whom I found the greatest frustration. These differences created tension in my ministry and produced unnecessary strife with those whom I was trying to lead. I was frustrated and confused on how to be an effective minister of the gospel because I held a faulty view of others, and myself, which led to poor relational skills. Thankfully, God brought me through the hindrances with a simple verse. I held fast to Psalm 139:14 (NIV): "I praise you because I am fearfully and wonderfully made; your works are wonderful, I know that full well."

Everyone has a God-given personality comprised of strengths and weaknesses. No one has a "bad" personality, and no personality type is better than another. The key element to successful leadership and effective ministry, I discovered, is what we do with our personalities. I believe once we understand our best personality traits and how to utilize our God-given strengths and talents, we can look upon others' traits, different as they may be, as strong suits, too. The discovery of my strengths and weaknesses has allowed me to gain a better understanding of how God created me and how he created others. This realization literally changed the way I function as a minister.

I believe each minister's skill set is built upon a foundation of our God-given personality. Each one of us has strengths and weaknesses intentionally designed by God, and each minister has a unique set of gifts, talents, and traits forming their personality and contributing to ministry effectiveness. God uses all types of personalities to complete his plan and purpose. I believe we are most effective when we choose to lead in situations that capitalize upon our strengths. Subsequently, we are least effective when we operate outside of our strength arena.

Ministering and leading people lends itself to a variety of challenges, but gaining an understanding of our core makeup and the personalities with which we have been graced by God enables us to experience great joy as we minister and lead people in each and every situation.

The understanding and recognition of one's weaknesses will allow for others to understand what to anticipate and how to assist in compensating for those weaknesses. For instance, if a person who is serving as a youth pastor is particularly weak in administrative abilities, then he or she should recruit lay leaders who can help compensate for this weakness. This recruitment and selection must also include the empowering of those individuals to utilize their strengths and the freedom which they may need to carry out a task.

This principle is a direct application of Paul's teaching in 1 Corinthians 12 and Romans 12 that each member of the body is important and gifted. And each member should be encouraged to use his or her gifts for the benefit of the whole with no jealousy or diminishing of another's giftedness.

ADDITIONAL RESOURCES

Fortune, Don, and Katie Fortune. *Discovering Your Children's Gifts.* Grand Rapids, MI: Chosen, 1989.

Fortune, Don, and Katie Fortune. *Discovering Your God-Given Gifts.* Grand Rapids, MI: Chosen, 1987.

Kise, Jane A. G., David Stark, and Sandra Krebs Hirsh. *LifeKeys.* Minneapolis, MN: Bethany House, 1996.

Trent, John, and Rodney Cox. *Leading From Your Strengths.* Nashville, TN: B & H Publishing Group, 2004.

6

PRINCIPLE SIX

Accept Your Limitations

Melissa had been raised in a pastor's home. Her father had pastored only two different churches in his forty-eight years of ministry. Melissa only experienced church life at First Baptist Church where her father was much-loved and respected. He was a multi-gifted man who saw the church experience consistent growth during his thirty-year ministry.

What Melissa didn't see was the frustration that he had experienced the last few years of his ministry as he had unconsciously developed a mentality among church members that the pastor must be the primary caregiver, teacher, leader, counselor, and more in the congregation. Consequently, this was Melissa's expectation of herself as she entered into ministry.

She had been called to serve as the minister of spiritual formation and Christian education for a large church. The leaders had recognized Melissa's gifts and strengths quickly. Soon, she was being asked to take on more responsibilities and to supervise the new youth pastor. The leaders assumed that Melissa would have no problem with this since she was so gifted, and single.

All went well until Melissa began to feel overwhelmed by these new responsibilities and began to neglect the oversight of her primary ministry areas. Her passion began to diminish and her frustration began to rise. She felt guilty because of her resentment, especially toward the new youth pastor.

Melissa had failed to accept her own limitations of time, energy, and leadership. She had assumed that a minister just accepted all that was asked of her to do.

A pastoral leader cannot be "superwoman" or "superman." Each leader has limitations of time, talents, and energy. The expectations of others must not set the agenda for the leader.

The material in this chapter is closely connected to that of the previous two chapters and also the following chapter. Accepting one's limitations assumes an understanding of one's strengths, a clear vision of one's core values, and an ability to maintain personal boundaries.

SELF-ACCEPTANCE AS KEY

One of the common challenges among ministry leaders is the acceptance of one's self with all the weaknesses that you bring to the leadership role. In many situations, expectations are so unrealistic concerning the role of the pastor that it adds to a sense of "unworthiness" on the part of the leader. This issue will be addressed more fully in chapter nine, but is certainly involved in this principle as well.

There is a tension in the understanding of "self-acceptance." It is *not* an encouragement to self-preoccupation or narcissism, rather to a healthy view of one's personhood in Christ. It could be dismissed as psychobabble in our "deistic therapeutic" evangelical world if it were not for the biblical truth that we are created by God as whole people. This includes physical, spiritual, intellectual, emotional, and social dimensions. "Ignoring any aspect of who we are as men and women made in God's image always results in destructive consequences—in our relationship with God, with others, and with ourselves."[1]

Unfortunately, many believers have attempted to ignore the relational or emotional aspects of their personal journeys. Denial of past wounds or rationalizing of emotional struggles with pious talk is not helpful. Experiencing wholeness through God's love and acceptance is a process.

Our spiritual enemy desires to discourage us with false messages that he will bring to our minds. It is a spiritual battle that can only be won through the power of the Word and the Spirit, in community with other Christians.

Scazzero correctly describes this battle and relates it to false messages that we have heard in our past as well as in our current culture in general:

> The sinister voices of the surrounding world and our pasts are powerful. They repeat the deeply held negative beliefs we may have learned in our families and cultures growing up:
>
> - I am a mistake.
> - I am a burden.
> - I am stupid.
> - I am worthless.
> - I am not allowed to make mistakes.
> - I must be approved of by certain people to feel okay.
> - I am valued based on my intelligence, wealth, and what I do, not for who I am.[2]

Only as we are willing to explore the interior of our souls can we fully experience the depth of God's grace and forgiveness. Again, Scazzero is a clear voice on this matter:

1. Scazzero, *Emotionally Healthy Spirituality*, 18.
2. Ibid., 53.

> Emotional health powerfully anchors me in the love of God by affirming that I am worthy of feeling, worthy of being alive, and lovable even when I am brutally honest about the good, the bad, and the ugly deep beneath the surface.[3]

There are many biblical truths that affirm our identity in Christ and that we are accepted, secure, and significant in Him! Just a few examples are: John 15:16; Romans 5:1; Romans 8:1–2; Ephesians 2:6, 10; Philippians 1:6; Colossians 1:13–14; and Colossians 2:9–10.

One of the most helpful books that I have discovered which presents a biblical perspective of our personhood is *The Gift of Being Yourself* by David Benner. Benner says:

> Our true self-in-Christ is the only self that will support authenticity. It and it alone provides an identity that is eternal.[4]

Many Christian leaders seek to create an identity through what they accomplish academically or professionally. It is often driven by the deep need for acceptance. This will become a burden too heavy to bear. Our "true self-in-Christ" is not earned, but it is given to us.

> Being most deeply your unique self is something that God desires, because your true self is grounded in Christ. God created you in uniqueness and seeks to restore you to that uniqueness in Christ. Finding and living out your true self is fulfilling your destiny.[5]

GOD'S "MASTERPIECE" FOR MINISTRY

One of the most radical statements in the New Testament about our nature apart from Christ is found in Ephesians 2. In the same

3. Ibid., 54.
4. Benner, *The Gift of Being Yourself*, 15.
5. Ibid., 16.

chapter is one of the strongest statements about God's amazing grace and His desire for us as we accept our "true self-in-Christ." Paul states that "we are his workmanship, created in Christ Jesus for good works" (verse 10). The Greek word translated "workmanship" is ποίημά. It may also mean "work of art" or "masterpiece." It is this deep truth that provides for us a sense of acceptance, not because of what we have or what we have done, but because of what God has done. He has created us anew in Christ. It is creation language here.

However, Paul goes on to tell us that it is not just for our own feelings of acceptance. It is that we might serve Christ as ministers to others. We serve from emotional and spiritual strength, not weakness. We thus give evidence to our new relationship with Jesus: "Good works are indispensable to salvation—not as its ground or means, however, but as its consequence and evidence."[6]

As new creatures in Christ, we are free to live out our faith honoring Christ by serving within healthy limits that flow from our inner life with Him. We faithfully and obediently serve him by serving others.

MOSES: LEADERSHIP LIMITS

The story of Moses in the Old Testament reveals a leadership journey filled with deep failures and exhilarating victories. It began with a loss of control and the rejection of his own people. It included a time of learning leadership principles from tending sheep. He came face-to-face with his own doubts and deficiencies before a burning bush. He learned lessons of dependency upon God as he confronted Pharaoh and as he led God's people out of bondage and to the Promised Land.

His father-in-law served as a mentor for him at a crucial point in his early leadership of the people of God as they began their journey. Jethro observed Moses judging the people and the drain upon his energy as the people were around him

6. Stott, *God's New Society*, 84–85.

all day (Exod 18:13). Jethro recognized that this was not a good situation for Moses or the people. He gave wise counsel to Moses. Moses respectfully listened, then followed the advice of his father-in-law. It seems reasonable to conclude that this was not the first time that Jethro had served in this mentoring role with Moses.

Jethro's counsel to Moses was that he needed to *accept his limitations*. The expectations of others should not determine his agenda and unrealistic demands should not diminish his sense of value.

In the account of his divine call through the burning bush (Exod 3,4), it appears that Moses struggled with a sense of inadequacy. God had to remind him that it was not about him, but the one whom he would serve. He needed to understand that the God who called him would be the God who would equip him for his leadership role. He would later learn that his weaknesses and limits would be used by God to expand the leadership of God's people.

When a Christian leader understands the God who calls, it is a freeing experience for him or her and a blessing to others who want to use their gifts. Personal limitations of time, talents, and energy should be viewed through the lens of God's call and provision.

GIFTS AND LIMITATIONS

Discovering one's spiritual gifts is not only a part of the process of discovering one's strengths, but also of accepting one's limitations. Paul's teaching in the specific passages mentioned in the previous chapter provide insight for accepting our limitations. Believers, including leaders, have been blessed by the Holy Spirit with gifts in order to function within the body of Christ. No one is to try to carry out every ministry alone, but to serve out of the gifts received. When this happens, the entire body will grow and be strengthened.

Acknowledging and accepting your leadership gifts and abilities with the limitations that go with them is actually encouraging to others within your ministry context. It helps them understand that they do not have to do everything and that they can be honest concerning their own limitations.

There is one particular *word of warning* that I want to give on this topic: never use your understanding of your strengths and gifts as an excuse to not meet pressing needs in ministry or to avoid some of the "dirtier" aspects of ministry. Leaders lead by example, and for a short time you will need to *simply serve* in a particular area. As you meet this need, you seek to recruit and equip others to serve in this area in the future.

RANDY HEMPHILL: LIMITS BRING FREEDOM

It was December of 2003, and our marriage had been dying a slow death. Eight years of ministry in four churches combined with academic pursuits led to a season that nearly destroyed our marriage. Let me be quick to say, ministry did not destroy our marriage. It was not the church's fault that our relationship collapsed. It was the unseen "crack in the Titanic," the emotional baggage of our lives that nearly sank us in ministry.

The irony of our story is that, at the time of collapse, I was the Marriage and Men's minister at a large, suburban church. Ministry had become my "drug of choice," my fountain of validation and worth. Being the son of a pastor, I remember feeling the draw to ministry at a young age. Church was the place where I felt close to my dad and felt validated as a young man. It was rewarding to deliver a sermon or meet a need. I had a need to be needed, the eternal "people-pleaser." All of this, combined with my wife's performance addiction and loneliness as a pastor's spouse, led us to a separation and near divorce.

What happened in 2004 and following is a story of grace, restoration, and *accepting limitations*. The flimsy scaffolding that we brought into marriage and ministry was finally dismantled, allowing God to rebuild us from the ground up ("humility" means to be grounded). We began a painful, fruitful journey of knowing God as Father and knowing self. Restoration in ministry and marriage hinges on these two truths. The whole process of restoration was framed with limitations.

The resiliency of a pastor's life lies in the process of accepting limitations. No one typically chooses limitations. In fact, we naturally do the opposite. Out of a sense of obligation to God and His church, we accept more responsibilities, take on a few more projects, agree to help more people, and commit to growing the church. All the while, pastors and their families get sacrificed on the altar of ministry.

When God allows or orchestrates brokenness in a pastor's life through burnout, ministry failure, heartache, or marital erosion, He wants to father you and me through a process of accepting our limitations. Limitations may include personality, gifting, season of life, life situations, wounds from the past, and emotional makeup. Brokenness creates opportunity for accepting limitations which ultimately leads to healthy pastors and healthy churches. And that is how limits bring freedom.

HONESTY IN COMMUNITY

This principle of resilience in ministry underscores again the importance of being involved in a community of truth and grace. Living and serving together in a community of healthy believers will encourage honesty in how leaders function within limits that respect their gifts, strengths, and time. Unhealthy and unrealistic expectations will be confronted, and the leader will be encouraged to lead as he or she has been called to lead. Limitations in the ministry of the church will be viewed through the lens of God's timing and provision.

ADDITIONAL RESOURCES

Allender, Dan B. *Leading With a Limp.* Colorado Springs, CO: WaterBrook, 2006.

Mulholland, M. Robert. *The Deeper Journey.* Downers Grove, IL: InterVarsity, 2006.

7

PRINCIPLE SEVEN

Maintain Boundaries

Tom was serving as the worship pastor of a large, growing congregation. He and his wife, Susan, had been married for seven years. Their four-year-old son, Jace, was a great joy in their lives. Susan worked at a local doctor's clinic as one of their staff RNs. For the past two years, she had arranged a four-day work schedule. Tom was working to complete his MA in Worship Ministry through an online program offered by his denomination's seminary.

Tom's weekdays usually began with him trying to catch a few minutes in prayer and Bible reading before his son awoke. His wife's schedule required her to leave their home by 6:30 a.m. each morning. As soon as Jace was up, the demands began. Tom helped get him ready, fed him breakfast, and took him to daycare by 8:00. Then, it was off to his office for full days of planning, meetings, and appointments. He and Susan alternated the pick-up schedule to get Jace from daycare. Two nights per week, Tom had to return to the church building for rehearsals with the worship team, choir, or soloists. On those evenings, Jace was already asleep when Tom returned home. Susan had arranged the four-day work schedule so they could all be home on Fridays.

In the past three months, Tom had only remained home all day on two Fridays. Most Fridays, he was going into his office or to the university library across town to work on his assignments for his online courses. Though he was home most Saturdays, his mind was on the services which he would be leading the next day. And regularly, he was getting phone calls from worship team members on Saturday who needed his attention.

Late one Thursday afternoon, Tom was in his office getting ready to leave to pick up Jace. As he sat staring out his office window, he began to cry. It quickly turned into full-blown sobbing. After gaining his composure, Tom began to evaluate the past year of his life. He had gained twenty pounds. He couldn't remember the last good night of sleep he had experienced. His physical intimacy with Susan was practically nonexistent. He and Jace had only had one "daddy/son" outing, and he couldn't remember the last time that he had been on the floor playing with Jace and his Legos. He felt deep resentment each semester when assignments came due for his online courses. He and his best friend from the church had not been together for weeks.

He realized that he was "running on empty" and that he could not maintain this schedule much longer. He needed to make some decisions, but he didn't know where to begin.

Maintaining clear boundaries is an important aspect of developing as a resilient leader. One's emotional, spiritual, mental, and physical well-being are dependent upon learning to address this need.

One of the most useful and practical resources for understanding and evaluating this area of boundaries is the highly acclaimed book by Henry Cloud and John Townsend, *Boundaries*. Though now over twenty years old, this book continues to provide wise counsel to leaders who want to serve effectively and finish well.

> In the physical world, boundaries are easy to see. . . . Physical boundaries mark a visible property line that *someone holds deed to*. . . . In the spiritual world, boundaries are just as real, but often harder to see. Boundaries define us. They define *what is me* and *what is not me*. A boundary shows me where I end and someone else begins, leading me to a sense of ownership. Knowing what I am to own and take responsibility for gives me freedom.[1]

Maintaining boundaries is not the same as shutting out or shutting down. Nor is it the same as neurotically keeping such a defined schedule that there is no room for pastoral sensitivity or crisis intervention. However, it does mean developing a strong sense of who I am and what my priorities should be and also embracing an important truth for ministry leaders: "I am responsible *to* my flock, but I am not responsible *for* every decision they make or action they take."[2]

The importance of understanding the universal nature of boundaries and their implications for the healthy functioning of people is clarified by Cloud and Townsend:

> God's world is set up with laws and principles. Spiritual realities are as real as gravity, and if you do not know them, you will discover their effects. Just because we have not been taught these principles of life and relationships does not mean they will not rule. We need to know the principles God has woven into life and operate according to them.[3]

Chapter Five of their book describes what they call the "Ten Laws of Boundaries." Understanding and applying these "laws" will bring a greater level of emotional, relational, and spiritual health for Christian leaders.

Many leaders find themselves working harder and maintaining fewer boundaries in their lives over time. Ministry activities

1. Cloud and Townsend, *Boundaries*, 29.

2. Gratitude to one of my supervisors in my DMin program, Dr. Robert Grizzard, for this helpful insight.

3. Cloud and Townsend, *Boundaries*, 84.

can begin to take the place of time with God or with one's family or time to refresh one's body.

SYMPTOMS OF A LIFE WITHOUT BOUNDARIES

Ignoring boundaries, or living without them, can have fatal consequences. One of the saddest testimonies concerning this issue is that of a great Christian pastor of the early 1800s, Robert Murray McCheyne, who died at age 29. McCheyne commented toward the end of his life, "God gave me the gospel and a horse. I've killed the horse, so I can no longer preach the gospel."[4] He was referring to his own body.

God created us as whole people—body, mind, soul. He wants us to use our whole selves to serve him and serve others, but not by devaluing our bodies. We cannot ignore God's example and instruction that rest and Sabbath are to be regular parts of our lives. To devalue the body and our care of it is a form of Gnosticism, which taught a dichotomy between the body and soul.

Stress is part of the life of the ministry leader. The story of Tom is repeated thousands of times in our ministry leadership world today. We cannot avoid all stress, but we can make some choices about boundaries that will help us minimize the stress.

> Stress is personal wear and tear associated with earning our living, caring for our families, Christian ministry, studying for exams, grieving for a loved one, and so on. Stress presents itself as tense muscles, increased blood pressure, disturbed digestion, increased metabolic rate and body temperature, disrupted sleep, restlessness, anxiety, guilt, feelings of helplessness and hopelessness, apathy, self pity, inefficiency, disorganization, indecisiveness, wishful thinking. The list goes on. But we don't just experience the stress of life; we also create it![5]

4. As quoted in Brain, *Going the Distance*, 20.

5. Cleary, "Coping With Stress," *Southern Cross* (1997), 15, quoted in Brain, *Going the Distance*, 40.

The list quoted above is one way of evaluating how one is experiencing stress. I have found that the list of questions below provide a helpful way to reflect upon my life and evaluate how I am doing with following my stated boundaries. As you read this list, take time to reflect upon the answers and the implications for your life:

- Are you able to rest or enjoy leisure activities?
- Are impatience and free-floating anger characterizing your reactions?
- Are you getting enough sleep? When you sleep, is it restful?
- Have you isolated yourself from any deep and honest relationships?
- Are you forgetting appointments?
- Is your devotional life consistent?
- Do you find yourself daydreaming in significant amounts of time?
- If married, does your spouse complain of loneliness or distance?
- Have your eating habits changed dramatically?
- Do you feel tired most of the time?

One other way of reviewing the symptoms of a life without boundaries is the helpful summary of symptoms discovered by researchers in the field of stress. They are: (1) a sense of being drained emotionally, (2) a reduced sense of personal accomplishment, and (3) a sense of depersonalization, of distance and disconnection in relationships.[6]

JOHN: BALANCING TRUTH AND LOVE

John, the apostle, had followed Jesus since his call by the shore of the Sea of Galilee. Along with his brother, James,

6. Brain, *Going the Distance*, 28.

and Peter, he was one of the members of the "inner circle" of Jesus. The gospels record various events in which these three are with Jesus on special occasions; one example is the Mount of Transfiguration.

John's faithfulness to Jesus and the close relationship they shared is evidenced by John's presence next to Jesus at the last supper, his staying near the cross, his running to see the empty tomb, and his leadership in the church after the resurrection. What we learn from the gospels and from John's own writings in the New Testament is that he was a man with a deep love for others, a sensitive spirit, a confidence in the Holy Spirit, an understanding of the process of discipleship, and a passion for truth.

John serves as a model for *maintaining boundaries* in one's walk with Christ. He had learned well from his Master. As we examine his letters to the believers across Asia Minor, we see a balanced emphasis on knowing Jesus, knowing oneself in Christ, loving others, and following the truth.

John had learned from the example and the teaching of Jesus that it is important to find times of rest and renewal in the midst of the stress of ministry. He had learned that body, soul, and spirit were all important to living a Spirit-filled life.

John's concern for his followers and their development is expressed in this verse in 3 John: "Beloved, I pray that all may go well with you and that you may be in good health, as it goes well with your soul." His letters are filled with a focus on the relationships of believers in the family of God and their commitment to truth, love, and abundant life in Jesus.

STRESS AND MINISTRY LEADERSHIP

Many ministry leaders are physically fatigued, emotionally drained, and spiritually empty. In our culture, change is accelerating, expectations on leaders are higher, and leadership is more demanding. Simultaneously, trust is lower. Simply put, "to lead is to live dangerously."[7]

Kevin Harney has stated the challenge faced by ministry leaders very succinctly:

> Leaders today seek to serve in the wake of countless moral failings, financial misdealing, lapses of integrity, and relational explosions of those who have gone before us. It's at our own peril that we press on with mindlessly busy schedules, resistance to accountability, and lifestyles that allow us no time to look into our own souls.[8]

In addition to these personal and interpersonal challenges, just the very nature of ministry leadership presents its own set of limitations and challenges. Here are fifteen particular factors that I observe related to the stress of ministry work:

1. The work of the church is never done
2. Unclear expectations by church lay leaders
3. Working with the same people through the various stages of life
4. The church is a haven for very needy people
5. Some individuals join a church because of a deep need for attention
6. The ministerial "persona"
7. Exhaustion from dealing with life "failures" (e.g., death, reversions, divorce)
8. Devaluation of the church and ministers by the general culture
9. Institutional decline in the culture
10. Poor time management in the church organization
11. Dealing with ambiguity

7. Heifetz and Linsky, *Leadership on the Line*, 2.
8. Harney, *Leadership from the Inside Out*, 13.

12. Demands on one's spouse and family
13. Constant threat of interpersonal conflict
14. Multiple "bosses"
15. Denominational politics

Each of these factors will add even more stress if the leader is not maintaining appropriate boundaries in his or her life.

Ministry leadership in the twenty-first century is difficult enough when the leader maintains appropriate boundaries that flow out of personal understanding of the biblical teaching about leaders. It can be impossible if one allows others in the church, or society in general, to determine the priorities of time and commitment.

Taking care of oneself as a leader is not being selfish. It is rather following God's desire that we be vital, fruitful leaders who serve in dependence upon him until our race is finished. Part of that dependence upon him means that we take the time to establish priorities for our work which have been bathed in prayer and spiritual reflection:

> A willingness to take every opportunity to articulate priorities will deliver immediate and long-term benefits to pastor and people. This of course presupposes that the pastor has some well thought out priorities for ministry. The pastor will be in a position of greater strength and understanding if these priorities have been worked through with the congregational leadership.[9]

SHAWN SHANNON: MAINTAINING BOUNDARIES THROUGH SABBATH

I was challenged to observe Sabbath when I read *Ordering Your Private World* by Gordon MacDonald. He distinguished between living as a *driven* person or as a *called* person. "Called people have strength from within, perseverance and

9. Brain, *Going the Distance*, 43.

power that are impervious to the blows from without." (52) He introduced the topic of Sabbath while speaking of the restoration of the minister's soul. Really? Was the Almighty coming to me to offer himself in fifty-two days per year dedicated to rest? Would God do that? Could I do that?

I began to explore Sabbath. I learned that the first entity scriptures name "holy" is time (Gen 2:3). I have heard that where there is the desire to learn, the teacher will appear. So it was that I began to hear of Sabbath and observe its practitioners all around me.

I became a committed "Sabbath attempter." The basic practice: I scan the week ahead for a 24-hour stretch when I will not lead or be responsible for something work-related. On that day (which is a Day Different, not a Day Off), I recalibrate my soul's compass. I shift from being a planner to being more spontaneous. I worship, take walks or naps, write in my journal. I fast from lists and email. I encourage those I serve to do the same.

This practice topples the idol I make of Productivity; I tend to believe that getting things done will purchase for me peace only God can provide. When I receive Sabbath, I am released from those twin drivers of fear ("Surely I will be left out, forgotten, or miss something!") and pride ("I am necessary to this ministry.")

A wise missionary friend of mine once said, "Shawn, it doesn't entirely depend on you." "It" equals all sorts of concerns of life. She was and is right. Keeping Sabbath is my affirmation that Someone Else runs the universe.

MAINTAINING BALANCE

Another perspective in considering the topic of boundaries is the need to maintain a balance in one's life. These areas of life balance as described in Appendix Four provide a template for setting priorities which address these various needs.

Fulfilling the Great Commandment to "love your neighbor as yourself" involves the matter of loving yourself correctly in order to love others healthily. Other ways to describe this would be "self-care" or "self-leadership." The danger in using such phrases is that some understand it to be a self-preoccupation or self-centeredness. And that can be an issue.

I would maintain that instead it is an application of the challenges which Paul gave to Timothy when he told Timothy to "train yourself for godliness" and "keep a close watch on yourself and on the teaching."[10]

ADDITIONAL RESOURCES

Brain, Peter. *Going the Distance.* Kingsford, Australia: Matthias Media, 2006.

Cloud, Henry, and John Townsend. *Boundaries: When to Say YES, When to Say NO.* Grand Rapids, MI: Zondervan, 1992.

London, H.B., and Neil B. Wiseman. *Pastors at Greater Risk.* Ventura, CA: Regal, 2003.

Wilson, Michael Todd, and Brad Hoffmann. *Preventing Ministry Failure.* Downers Grove, IL: InterVarsity, 2007.

10. 1 Tim 4: 7, 16.

8

PRINCIPLE EIGHT

Maintain Emotional Stability

Gary was the administrative pastor of a large church in the largest city in the state. The reputation of the church and the senior pastor were well-known throughout the city and state. Gary considered this to be his "dream" position and was convinced that it fit him perfectly.

All went well for two years, and Gary was viewed as a success in his role by his peers on staff and by the church. What his peers could not see was the turmoil inside Gary. Gary's father was a very controlling, demanding man. Gary had always tried to meet his father's unrealistic expectations. But in his own heart, he felt that he had always fallen short. These feelings were exacerbated when Gary left business school and entered seminary against his father's wishes.

The senior pastor in this church had been there for several years prior to Gary's acceptance of his position. The senior pastor had experienced great success in leading this congregation from being a very small one to one with multiple ministries and with a multiple staff. Gary was the first person to serve as administrative pastor.

Initially, Gary and the senior pastor had a good working relationship. Then, after two years in this ministry, Gary had an "explosion." His wife noticed that he was increasingly irritable when he came home and that he never seemed content. He also began to criticize the senior pastor, first at home, then even to some other staff members and church members.

The "explosion" occurred at a Monday morning staff meeting after a particularly stressful weekend of ministry activities which had required Gary's attention. The senior pastor asked Gary about one of these activities and Gary perceived it as a criticism. Gary lost control, even swearing at the senior pastor. His reaction was disproportionate to the issue at hand. The senior pastor responded with his "control mode" and an ugly scene ensued. Gary was eventually asked to leave the meeting and the senior pastor said they would meet the next morning. Gary went home and unloaded on his wife who was hurt and confused.

Fortunately for Gary, one of the other staff members who had been with the church for several years was an insightful individual who met with Gary that evening to process the event. He helped Gary understand that there was more going on inside him than just what happened at the meeting. Through his advice and encouragement, Gary began to meet with a counselor. His ministry was saved, his relationship with his senior pastor was restored, and his marriage became more fulfilling.

Unfortunately, similar experiences occur frequently in the lives of Christian leaders, and irreparable damage is done to relationships and ministries. These times of "explosion" (internal and external) have the potential to become a time of greater self-understanding if the leader is willing to invest in personal reflection and to process the "explosion" with a trusted friend or counselor.

If the leader does not take some personal responsibility and only engages in blaming others, or circumstances, the scenario is certain to be played out again. A proactive approach to self-understanding and learning to maintain emotional stability is preferable. Rather than being sabotaged by one's reactions, it is possible to know what personal issues are growing "edges," what situations tend to trigger one's defenses, and what is one's emotional "default" condition. Spending time to invest in self-awareness will pay great dividends for a leader. This was true for me personally as I was involved in one-on-one and small group reflection experiences in my doctoral program in pastoral counseling. It was during that time that I came to embrace in a healthier manner my early formation experiences in my family of origin and the impact upon my leadership.

UNDERSTANDING OUR JOURNEY

All Christian leaders have been shaped by the collective experiences of their lives. Our personal journeys may have included many "detours" along the way or even begun with significant challenges as a result of our circumstances. These experiences do not qualify or disqualify us to serve as leaders in God's kingdom. They *do not determine us* or our contributions to the lives of others. However, the experiences of our journey do shape and influence us in significant ways that are important to understand if we want to be healthy, mature leaders and effective servant-leaders with others.

This understanding of our journey will provide benefits for our family relationships, personal relationships with friends and colleagues, as well as growth in our leadership abilities. Reggie McNeal states pointedly and insightfully the value of spending time to examine and understand our journey:

> The most important information you will need as a leader—*self-understanding.* This is a different issue than self-preoccupation. Self-preoccupation shows up in leaders who use others in order to achieve their own ambitions. Self-understanding begins and ends with God. This takes time and reflection. However, I am convinced that the most effective leaders are those who take time to ponder what God is up to in their own lives. Those who understand their own hearts will be better prepared to

> lead amid the growing discontinuities at the dawn of the third Christian millennium.[1]

John Calvin has a statement which can help keep us "God-focused" as we review our personal journey:

> Man never attains to a true self-knowledge until he has previously contemplated the face of God, and come down after such contemplation to look into himself . . . so long as we do not look beyond the earth, we are quite pleased with our righteousness, wisdom, and virtue, we address ourselves in the most flattering terms, and seem only less than demigods. . . . Men are never duly touched and impressed with their insignificance, until they have contrasted themselves with the majesty of God.[2]

Many of us have recognized the hand of God at work through our early years of life and the various relationships which we enjoyed or endured. There are two particular tools which will be described that are helpful in exploring the life experiences in one's journey. These tools assist the leader to "look in the rearview mirror as you face forward."[3]

Personal Life Map

The Personal Life Map provides an exercise for reflecting upon one's journey in a structured manner utilizing particular shaping influences from one's past. Appendix Five provides a template for the Personal Life Map exercise.

This reflection exercise involves breaking one's life into seven-year segments. As you complete the template, positive shaping experiences are noted above the dotted line and negative experiences are noted below the dotted line.

Appendix Six (Heart Shaping Factors) provides a visual representation of eight subplots that may be utilized as one reflects

1. McNeal, *A Work of Heart*, xiv–xv.
2. Calvin, *Institutes*, 37–39.
3. Cole, *Journeys to Significance*, 13.

upon the various shaping experiences. This is adapted from material by Reggie McNeal in his book, *A Work of Heart.*

Through this exercise the leader will gain a clearer perspective on his or her life experiences and how God has used both positive and negative experiences to mold character or equip for leadership. Also, chronic problematic areas in relationships or leadership style may be surfaced and then can be addressed in a healthy manner. Ultimately, you will see evidence of God's grace and faithfulness in your life.

The journey inward can become very painful for some. It may even require a time of inviting a professional counselor to assist in the journey and in the discovery of healing for past hurts, forgiveness for past sins, and reconciliation for broken relationships. The journey requires time and effort. It may occasionally inflict great pain. Perhaps this is why many choose not to make the journey. But the cost in the long run of not taking this journey is often more than the cost of taking it now. As the late Dag Hammarskjold said, "The longest journey of any person is the journey inward."

Johari Window

The Johari Window was a technique developed by Joseph Luft and Harrington Ingham. It has been used for decades as an exercise to help people better understand their relationship with self and with others. There is a list of adjectives which are commonly used for the exercise by the individual and a group of peers. This list is available on various websites.

Appendix Seven provides the template of the Johari Window and its four quadrants: Blind Self, Unknown Self, Hidden Self, and Open Self. In addition, I have included a description of the individual or individuals who would be necessary to assist one in moving some areas of self-understanding from one quadrant to another.

While there will be certain experiences or interpersonal dynamics which should remain in a particular quadrant, the overall goal is to move much of our self-understanding into the light of the "Open Self." This will involve the practice of confession, confrontation, submission, truthfulness, and forgiveness. The deepest areas of transparency should be communicated only in the context of deep trust, love, and confidentiality.

SOLOMON: WISDOM AND FOOLISHNESS

Unlike his father, Solomon grew up in the context of wealth and power. He was well-educated and saw both the glory and the dangers of privilege. During his youth, Israel was a united nation and was growing in power.

Solomon's accession to David's throne was filled with intrigue and conflict. After all, Solomon was not the oldest son. However, he was God's choice. He would be the man who would oversee the building of God's temple. The construction of the temple and its dedication reveal some of the depth of Solomon's spiritual journey.

When given an opportunity to ask God for anything, Solomon chose well and asked for wisdom. God was pleased and showed great favor to Solomon. His wisdom was legendary. The book of Proverbs contains much of Solomon's wisdom.

However, later in life, it became clear that Solomon was moving away from his close relationship with God. The wise one became foolish. He sought to secure his power through his own schemes and failed to *maintain emotional stability*. His growing instability revealed a lack of reliance on God and a growing appetite for sex and power. His many wives worshipped other gods and turned his heart from worshipping the true God. He appeared to suffer through times of disillusionment and discouragement.

Solomon could have benefitted from a wise counselor who would have helped him to understand his journey and uncover hidden areas of his life. Perhaps, his history of privilege, wealth, and power were his undoing. He was not an example of spiritual integrity in the end.

UNDERSTANDING AND CONFRONTING BARRIERS TO MATURITY

The psalmist cried out to God: "Search me, O God, and know my heart! Try me and know my thoughts! And see if there be any grievous way in me, and lead me in the way everlasting!" (Ps 139:23–24).

The apostle Paul was concerned for the personal growth of his two protégés, Timothy and Titus. A review of the letters he sent to them reveals many exhortations to pay attention to their lives and to consider their pasts so that their witness may not be hindered and that their ministry may be fruitful.

There are two tools described in this section which can also provide deeper self-understanding in order to confront any barriers which might be hindering the leader's growth and maturity.

Genogram

Each person is unique, having been shaped by a combination of nature, nurture, and life experiences. Undoubtedly, one's family of origin is the most significant shaping community one experiences. "It is clear that our family experience during our young, dependent years shapes and sculpts who we become to a considerable degree."[4]

An important place to begin in understanding our family of origin and our place in that family is to create a genogram. A genogram (also called a "family diagram" by some authors) is a diagrammatic method for depicting multiple generations in one's family of origin for the purpose of gaining a better understanding of emotional processes which have shaped the individual.

A genogram is not the same as a family tree. The genogram reflects the emotional processes through the generations and is most useful as the principles of family systems theory are applied. It provides a tool for deeper reflection and discussion for the individual.

4. Gilbert, *Extraordinary Leadership*, 33.

Excerpts of a paper presented for the Association of Doctor of Ministry Education (ADME) by Mark Searby and Susan Goble are included as Appendix Eight. This appendix provides a more detailed rationale and description of the genogram. Also, Appendix Nine includes a list of questions developed by Peter Scazzero to utilize in gaining a better understanding of how one has been shaped by various issues from the family of origin.

Reading and Reflection

Appendix Ten is a paper written by Dr. John Walker, founder and director of Blessing Ranch Ministries in New Port Richey, Florida. Blessing Ranch is a ministry primarily to hurting clergy and their spouses. Walker identifies three types of "serious wrecks" in leadership ministry and the signs of their inner pain which are manifested in their outward ministry. He also provides suggestions for how to help these three types of leaders.

Reading and processing this paper provides another means for seeking self-knowledge. Dr. Walker's concluding paragraph says: "The process of blending emotional and spiritual growth for significant Christian leaders often involves *intentional collegiality* that gives perspective, challenges, finds creative solutions and 'walks in the soul' of the other along the path of God" (italics mine).

RICK GRACE: REFLECTIVE PASTOR

One of the best known works of John Calvin is his *Institutes of the Christian Religion*. What is less known is that Calvin started the *Institutes* in 1536 as a small treatise to introduce theological students to the Bible. It did not take its final voluminous form until 1559. Over those thirty-three years, it was revised and expanded numerous times. As Calvin also wrote commentaries on nearly every biblical book during those three decades, his reflection on Scripture shaped and reshaped his

Institutes. His life models one who did not just evaluate things but who learned the discipline of theological reflection.

Evaluation is often focused solely on the results of whatever effort is being examined, the primary question being, "Did it work to bring about the desired results?" In the church world, that usually means how many people participated, were there significant decisions made for Christ, and ironically, yet often seemingly most important, did we come in under budget? Those are all fine questions to raise—if you are simply evaluating the impact of an event.

Theological reflection is focused more on the biblical principles and theological categories involved. The primary question becomes, "Was God blessed by what we did?" Reflection helps to identify consistency to our sense of mission, our values, and the timeless truths we are trying to reinforce to the people of God. Reflection shapes and reshapes our interaction with the Word and the world around us.

Grasping the difference has made a qualitative impact in my life. I still ask the first set of questions as part of the evaluative process. That is a necessary component of faithfully shepherding the church God has entrusted to me. But I now pay much more attention to who was developed in the process, whose walk with the Lord was strengthened, and who learned a valuable lesson of discipleship or leadership. Reflection asks if what was just done is consistent with the trajectory of Scripture and our congregational calling. What story was just told about who we are as a church family, and how does our little story fit into the one large story of redemption told in Scripture? Without the discipline of theological reflection, ministry would be lacking a key component that leads to the richness of seeing how we are fitting into the meta-narrative of God reclaiming the world for His own glory.

CONCLUDING THOUGHTS ON MAINTAINING EMOTIONAL STABILITY

The concepts in this chapter may be new to many leaders and may be received as unnecessary. I would ask that you suspend judgment until you have engaged the exercises.

I have been amazed by discoveries made by students who have completed a three-generation genogram. One of the most profound discoveries involved multigenerational depression and suicide among the males of one family.

A leader will gain the most from these exercises if they are shared in a small group, with a trusted colleague, or with a counselor. In these contexts, questions can be asked and gentle probing accomplished to assist in greater insight and application. Deep-seated feelings which have been buried may come up in these activities and can then be processed in a safe environment.

ADDITIONAL RESOURCES

Gilbert, Roberta M. *Extraordinary Leadership.* Falls Church, VA: Leading Systems, 2006.

Richardson, Ronald W. *Becoming a Healthier Pastor.* Minneapolis, MN: Fortress, 2005.

Scazzero, Peter. *The Emotionally Healthy Church.* Grand Rapids, MI: Zondervan, 2003.

Steinke, Peter L. *How Your Church Family Works.* Herndon, VA: The Alban Institute, 2006.

9

PRINCIPLE NINE

Reject Erroneous Messages

Kevin was the pastor of a small, rural church which averaged approximately sixty-five in attendance each Sunday. He had accepted the call to this church after serving for six years as the associate pastor at a large church which was located three hours south of his current context. He and his wife had struggled with the decision to make this transition. They would be serving in a much smaller context, and he would be taking a cut in salary. His peers on staff at the large church told him that he was making a mistake and it would hurt his chances for future ministry in better churches.

After much prayer, Kevin and his wife had decided to accept the call. It was now three years into this ministry, and they both were confident that this is where God wanted them to be. But it was not without days of questioning his value and the value of his ministry.

It seemed that almost every denominational magazine highlighted the large "successful" ministries in its pages. All of the conferences he attended had keynote speakers and workshop leaders from "thriving" ministries. At one of the conferences, his successor in his last ministry was one of the main speakers!

Kevin had quit counting the number of times one of his members referred to Andy Stanley or Tim Keller or Rick Warren. He was thankful for two other pastors in his area with whom he met regularly. They could laugh together about who had heard the most references to a famous preacher in the past month.

The toughest day came when one of his members announced to him that he was leaving and going to the larger church in a nearby city. Kevin had spent hours with this man as he watched his wife die from her second bout with cancer. He had been in one of Kevin's small groups and seemed to really appreciate their relationship. Kevin could not help but wonder, "Does my ministry make any difference?"

One other "demon" that haunted him from time to time was his recollection of turning down a full-ride scholarship to medical school and choosing to go to seminary instead. Where would he be now if he had chosen that path?

This story is repeated many times daily, especially with the leaders of smaller churches or bivocational pastors. There are many messages which get communicated to Christian leaders; some are blatant and some more subtle. It is important to learn how to weigh those messages and, in many cases, to simply reject them.

It appears to me that there are three primary sources for the erroneous messages which bombard pastors: the devil, the culture, and other Christians. Some of these messages are direct attacks on the pastor's psyche, and some take the form of measuring the "success" of one's ministry.

SATAN AS ACCUSER AND DECEIVER

Our spiritual enemy is the great deceiver and accuser. Throughout the scriptures, we read of this enemy who seeks to destroy God's people in any way possible and wants to detract them from fulfilling God's purposes. Satan will twist the truth for his own purposes, seeking to destroy God's work and God's people.

J. I. Packer has some great insights about the devil's efforts to thwart the work of godly leaders in his book on Nehemiah:

> The real theme of Nehemiah 4–6 is spiritual warfare, and Nehemiah's real opponent, lurking behind the human opponents, critics, and grumblers who occupied his attention directly, was Satan, whose name means "adversary" and who operates as the permanent enemy of God, God's people, God's work, and God's praise.[1]

Leaders should expect opposition from without. Our enemy will use circumstances and people as his instruments to seek to deceive us or make us doubt our ministry or ourselves.

Continuing in his exposition of Nehemiah, Packer states:

> We turn now to the three types of attack that Satan used his human agents to mount against Nehemiah's great team of builders. There was psychological warfare, there were physical threats, and there were personal discouragements and underminings.[2]

Nehemiah did not allow the enemy or his agents to destroy his team of workers or himself. Through faithful devotion to God and tireless work, they completed their task to God's glory. They persevered through the emotional and physical threats.

When we turn to the New Testament for examples, Jesus stands as a model of how to win the victory against the Accuser. In Luke 4, we read about the encounter between Jesus and Satan as Jesus began his ministry. He did not allow the lies and truth-twisting of Satan to deter him from his mission, which had been given to him by the Father.

The apostles and the early church were attacked from within by the enemy. He used Ananias and Sapphira as instruments of deceit to try to destroy the church's witness. He used grumbling and discontent by the Hellenist widows to try to destroy their unity.

1. Packer, *A Passion for Faithfulness*, 93.
2. Ibid., 99.

When these attacks did not work, the enemy sought to destroy the ministry of the church through physical persecution (Acts 8:1). The result of this persecution was that the church actually grew and expanded its witness as the leaders and many believers faithfully served God through the power of the Holy Spirit. Historically, the church has grown in times of persecution, and the growth of the church in China is one recent example.

Paul recognized that the followers of Christ would come under spiritual attack. In his letters, he warned the leaders particularly, and all believers generally, that they were in a spiritual battle. Paul's letter to the Ephesians is very instructive about spiritual warfare, especially in light of the history of the city and the church founded there (cf. Acts 19).

> Paul knew Satan wouldn't give up the battle. If the devil couldn't threaten Christ believers with fear of suffering and death, then he would use other "schemes" to try to subvert the work of Christ. If he couldn't win the fight using a frontal assault (worry, fear, suffering, and death cannot penetrate the armor of Christ), then he would get Christ believers to fight one another, stabbing each other in the back.[3]

Out of the insights and growth from his own experiences of spiritual warfare, Paul challenged the believers to trust in Christ and his work for them. He challenged them to put on the armor which would help them win the battles (Eph 6:10–18a).

> This is where we need to be very clear about how Paul saw the armor of Christ work as protection against evil powers. Paul never claimed that bad things would never happen to Christ believers. . . . Rather, Paul claimed that his converts would be able to face the difficulties of life by standing firm in their faith. The point is *not* that Christ believers never get sick or never get hurt or never die as long as they're wearing the armor of Christ. Instead, wearing the resurrection of Christ like body armor helps

3. Reeves, *Spirituality According to Paul*, 213.

> believers stand during hard times in the strength of the Lord's power (Eph 6:10).[4]

This same accuser is alive and well today. He will use all means at his disposal to discourage and defeat Christian leaders. He uses "human agents" as his instruments at times. He will use the emotional, relational, and spiritual weak points of any leader as places of attack. Satan will twist words that we hear so that we hear them as erroneous messages of deprecation or defeat. We must resist these attacks in the power of the Holy Spirit.

As I stated in Chapter Three, the resilient pastor affirms that we are in a spiritual battle and that there are times when the battle is very intense. In these times, we need special reliance on the spiritual armor, prayer, and the encouragement of fellow believers. "We who are Christ's should detest Satan but not dread him, since God now provides us with all-purpose combat equipment for use against him."[5]

PETER: FRUITFUL SHEPHERD

As he neared the end of his life, the apostle Peter wrote two letters that are included in our canon today. These two letters were written by a seasoned leader to believers who were being treated with contempt and, in many cases, persecuted. He could identify with them on a very personal level, as he had experienced what they were going through.

Peter's letters reveal an honest appraisal of the challenges without turning fatalistic. He did not want them to underestimate the enemy. He did want them to grow in their trust in "the God of all grace."

Peter knew that these believers were facing tremendous obstacles and receiving falsehoods from without and within. He encouraged them to *reject the erroneous messages* with which they were being bombarded. He encouraged them to

4. Ibid., 210.

5. Packer, *A Passion for Faithfulness*, 95.

stand firm in the true grace of God and to "grow in the grace and knowledge of our Lord and Savior Jesus Christ."[6]

It is impossible to read Peter's letters and not think of his own journey which was littered with failures. He had succumbed many times to the lies of the enemy. He had been sifted and yet found faithful in the end. His own experiences of grace and restoration are reflected in his counsel to these young Christians.

The spirit of Peter's exhortations is found in his own self-designation as a "fellow elder" with the elders/shepherds of the church. The shepherding imagery reminds us of Peter's own restoration and the challenge he received from Jesus on that beach some thirty years before. A leader will serve as a shepherd to guard the flock against its enemies. The shepherd guards and feeds those in his care. The true shepherd will even lay down his life for the sheep if necessary.

CHALLENGES FROM CONTEMPORARY CULTURE

Leaders in churches in North America face very complex and confusing conditions in the current social and religious context. The challenges presented by changing social values and the demands of technology bring a new set of issues which leaders must address while seeking to be faithful to their call to ministry.

The voices from contemporary culture will bring many erroneous messages to the hearts and minds of pastoral leaders. Demands will be placed upon these leaders which need to be evaluated in light of biblical teaching.

The words of Will Willimon provide a clear warning to emerging Christian leaders as they seek to discern the ministry to which they are being called:

> One of the challenges of the ordained ministry is to find those metaphors for ministry that allow us appropriately to embody the peculiar vocation of Christian leadership.

6. 2 Pet 3:18.

> Uncritical borrowing from the culture's images of leadership can be the death of specifically *Christian* leaders.[7]

Willimon further points out that some of the popular contemporary metaphors are: media mogul, political negotiator, therapist, manager, and resident activist.[8] These metaphors can take a leader far from the biblical principles and perspectives on leadership.

Even though it would be difficult to find a consensus among biblical teachers and leaders concerning the essential metaphors of ministry which should provide direction for emerging leaders, most would agree that Christian leaders should be *Christ-centered*, *Spirit-directed*, *Word-focused*, and *People-oriented*. This type of leader would not be program-driven or organizationally motivated, but rather kingdom-oriented and pastorally sensitive. The two primary biblical metaphors for leaders—*shepherds* and *servants*—would satisfy this need.

Many of the erroneous messages from the culture which bombard Christian leaders relate to success, popularity, power, and inclusiveness.[9] It takes a strong, healthy image of one's "self-in-Christ" to resist many of these messages. As is typical of many of the enemy's ploys, good things are twisted to become the center of work instead of a part of our work. A helpful resource to critique this area of leadership and ministry is a chapter in a recent book by one of my colleagues, Doug Webster. The chapter is entitled "Christ *for* Culture."[10]

CHALLENGES FROM CHRISTIANS

Unfortunately, some of the strongest erroneous messages come from other Christian leaders. Many of these come unintentionally and even subtly. It generally reveals the spiritual and/or emotional

7. Willimon, *Pastor*, 55.

8. Ibid., 56–66.

9. While we are to be welcoming and non-judgmental in our ministries, we must not surrender our biblical and theological foundations.

10. Webster, *Living in Tension*, 1–29.

insecurities of the one who speaks the message but unfortunately fosters an atmosphere of competition or suspicion.

Many of these challenges come in the form of comparison: comparing one leader's success or pedigree to another's. If you serve a large church, or if you have an advanced degree, then you are judged to be qualitatively better than the other person. If you are receiving requests to speak in other churches or at conferences, then you must be better than those who do not. It is the same principle which Paul addressed in 1 Corinthians 3 as he confronted the Corinthians with their "personality worship."

The tension here is the honest recognition of an individual's giftedness without praising the gift in place of the Giver. Another tension is giving the glory to God when good things are taking place in one's ministry (including numerical growth) and feeling good about how he has chosen to use the individual leader.

Some of those most guilty in propagating these erroneous messages are pastors themselves. I have yet to attend a church or leadership conference where the comparison game is not rampant. In some cases, it can be sickening to watch Christian leaders who are more concerned that everyone know who they are and what they have accomplished than they are that there are fellow leaders who are struggling or suffering.

It is a true gift from God when a pastor can be part of a small group of other pastors who truly care about one another and desire that each be fruitful in his or her ministry. I experienced such a gift in my last pastoral ministry. We had a group of evangelical pastors in our community who met regularly to share and pray for one another. We were all from different denominations, but there was no competition or comparison. We helped carry one another's burdens and rejoiced when others experienced victories.

However, these challenges do not come only from other pastors or leaders. They often come from well-meaning church members. With the proliferation of media in our culture, the ministries of prominent churches and leaders are highlighted in many ways. Worship services and sermons are available on TV, radio, and on the Web in many forms. The quality of most of these services and sermons is excellent. These then become the standard of measurement by which many Christians judge their congregation and their pastors. These new tools for ministry need to be viewed in the proper perspective, as supplemental for a believer's education and growth, but never used to compare the ministry of another. I honestly believe that most church members have no clue that their comments can be so hurtful or discouraging to their own leader or leaders who are trying to be faithful with the resources they have in the context to which God has called them.

In order to resist these erroneous messages from other Christians, the leader must have a strong, biblical perspective on his or her own personhood and call. Also, the leader must seek to be in regular fellowship with other leaders who share this understanding.

JASON MCCONNELL: FAITHFUL SERVANT

Just out of seminary, I accepted a call to pastor a little white-steeple country church in the mountains of northern Vermont. The landscape was gentle and picturesque: the rolling green hills were dotted with red barns, black and white Holstein cows, and hard-working "salt-of-the-earth" people. The whole scene portrayed a picture of peace and tranquility from a simpler life of bygone days.

The first few months of ministry were delightful! Church attendance was high, the worship services flowed effortlessly, sermons were received with unexpected enthusiasm, and my wife and I enjoyed the gifts of hospitality and good food from many faithful parishioners. Even the broader community outside the church seemed genuinely grateful for our presence in town. They referred to me as "my pastor" even if they never darkened the doors of the church. We rejoiced that the Lord called us to such a wonderful place with such a lovely people.

But the honeymoon came to an abrupt end one day when I stopped by the home of the chairman of the deacon board, a man who had been a member of the church for more than fifty years. After a brief visit, he smiled and said, "I am glad that you came by today; I have something that I want to talk to you about." Then he handed me a list of taboo sermon topics and said, "Vermont is a politically liberal state, so we don't want to hear any sermons on these subjects." The list contained a host of controversial social issues and a few uncomfortable theological themes.

Even if he was the resident patriarch of the church, I was shocked by his audacity to unilaterally censor my sermon choices. I thought to myself, "Who do you think you are to question my pastoral authority?" What made it worse was that he refused to give me any specific reasons why these topics were out-of-bounds. My anger and frustration caused me to wonder if I had ended up in the right place. I asked myself, "Was this really God's call or was it Satan's trap? Is this some type of Abrahamic test of faith? Can I stay in a situation like this?

I had a decision to make, and I had to make it quickly. In that moment, God gave me the grace to resist my natural instincts to react to his verbal affront. Instead, I calmly explained that none of those issues were my personal hobby-horses, but that as an expository preacher, I would not avoid them when they appeared in the Scriptures. I chose to put on the armor of God and endure the erroneous messages of the evil one.

Over the past ten years, as I have learned more about the ministry context and earned credibility from the congregation, I have addressed every one of those topics from the pulpit. At the end of a sermon on one of those controversial subjects, the deacon patted me on the back and said, "Well done!" I am so glad that the Lord led me to choose the path of resilience!

WHAT IS "EXCELLENT" MINISTRY?

One of the antidotes to the discouragement which comes from accepting the erroneous messages which come to leaders is a clear, balanced understanding of what it means to carry out excellence in one's ministry. Jones and Armstrong have observed that "excellence has become the Holy Grail of American culture."[11]

Churches and Christian leaders often adopt worldly understandings of "excellence." So, is it even possible to use this word without bringing all the cultural baggage with it? As Jones and Armstrong argue in their book, I believe that we can speak of excellent ministry if the primary criterion is "fidelity to the crucified and risen Christ."[12]

> Excellent ministry is the presence and power of the Triune God being manifested in a person's life and leadership.

The words excellent and excellence come from the Latin word "excello," meaning "to rise above, surpass." So, what is the Christian leader to rise above? He or she is to rise above the ways of the world, lukewarmness/mediocrity, and one's own abilities and reason. It does *not* mean to rise above other leaders.

Excellent ministry as defined above is Christocentric. The Christological and pastoral foundation for this kind of ministry can be found in Colossians 1:3–14 and 24–29! In summary of this passage, I would say that leadership excellence is doing something by faith in Christ with a deep commitment to giving your best at all times with a goal that is other-directed.

When we consider how culture has shaped much of the current definition of excellence (read "success"), we see the following instruments used in measuring ministry success:

- attendance
- budget
- large staff
- busyness
- salary
- popularity/recognition

11. Jones and Armstrong, *Resurrecting Excellence*, 1.

12. Ibid., 7.

- external speaking engagements

Do not misunderstand, we should be concerned about the health and vitality of our leadership and our churches. We should care deeply that spiritual transformation is occurring in our context. However, the prevailing, culturally shaped metrics which are utilized should not be the primary ones. "To be sure, the criteria by which we ought to measure Christian life will be qualitative as well as quantitative, and thus difficult to summarize."[13]

Excellent ministry will be found in a variety of circumstances and contexts: a rural church of seventy members who are touching the elderly in their community, an inner city church plant that meets in one of the local nightclubs, a suburban church that has a significant outreach to HIV patients, a medium size church in the South that has been faithfully winning the lost to Jesus for years, and a mega church that has over 500 college students in their worship services each Sunday.

The danger is that any one of these churches, or leaders of these churches, could become more worried about evaluating the other's ministry than their own. An example that I have witnessed is when members of smaller churches begin casting stones at mega churches while they "settle for mediocrity masquerading as faithfulness."[14]

Each leader and each ministry must conduct regular self-evaluation to discern the overall health and practice of excellence in its context, asking questions about being Christocentric. While acknowledging the danger of lists, I would like to provide the following to utilize in examining the "being" and "doing" aspects of ministry for leaders. Scriptures are provided for each characteristic or practice:

13. Ibid., 6.

14. This statement is attributed to John Wimmer by Jones and Armstrong, Ibid., 2.

Excellent ministers are characterized by (Being):

- Faithfulness—2 Tim 4:7; 1 Cor 4:2
- Service—1 Cor 4:1; Phil 2; John 13
- Humility—1 Cor 2:1–5; 1 Pet 5:5
- Prayer—Eph 1:15–23; Eph 6:18–20; 1 Tim 2:1–2
- Holiness—1 Tim 4:12; 6:11–12
- Love—John 13:35; Rom 12:10; 1 Thess 3:11–13
- Passion (for God and for people)—Mark 12:30–31; Col 1:28–29

Excellent ministers practice (Doing):

- Spiritual Disciplines—Luke 5:16; John 15:1–11; Acts 2:42; 2 Pet 3:18
- Self-Care—Prov 4:23; 1 Tim 4:16
- Study of the Word—2 Tim 2:15, 3:16
- Utilization of personal giftedness—1 Tim 4:14–15; 2 Tim 1:6–7
- Equipping others for ministry—Eph 4:11–16
- Involvement in mentoring relationships—Mark 3:14; 2 Tim 2:2

All we do should be an act of worship to the Most Excellent One!

ADDITIONAL RESOURCES

Eswine, Zack. *Sensing Jesus.* Wheaton, IL: Crossway, 2013.
Reeves, Rodney. *Spirituality According to Paul.* Downers Grove, IL: IVP Academic, 2011.
Sisk, Ronald D. *The Competent Pastor.* Herndon, VA: The Alban Institute, 2005.
Tripp, Paul David. *Dangerous Calling.* Wheaton, IL: Crossway, 2012.

10

PRINCIPLE TEN

Embrace Grace

Larry was amazing! As I listened to his story, I kept saying, "really," or "you're making this up," or "you should be dead." But the whole story was true! Larry had lived in the pit of drugs and despair, but now walked in the fullness of God's amazing grace.

When I met him, Larry had been serving as a pastor in a medium size church for four years. He was married and had two children, a girl and a boy. His faith was vital and his spirit contagious. His warm smile and quick laughter were encouraging to all around him. His church members loved him and respected him.

It had only been about seven years prior that Larry woke up one morning in the back seat of his car (which served as his home) after a night of drinking and smoking pot, with a woman who had been his "live-in" girlfriend for a few months. It was that day that he heard the voice of God saying that it was not too late to change his life, if he would embrace God's grace. He left his girlfriend, asked his parents if they would take him back (he was 34 at the time), and began attending church. In a few months, Larry sensed that God was calling him to become a pastor and wanted him to go to seminary. It was a tough road, but he finished seminary, met his wife, and accepted a call to serve this church.

Larry continues to live in awe of God's wonderful, amazing grace, and he extends that grace passionately to those in his church and his community. He is solidly biblical in his teaching and preaching, but presents it in a way that draws others in with a desire to experience the same change that they know Larry has experienced.

Larry's story is dramatic and not so common. However, it is a tremendous illustration of God's grace and its power to transform lives, even those who have experienced much sin and despair.

In leadership, every leader must learn this important principle of resilience, for every leader will experience times of failure. In those times, we must embrace the grace that is offered by our heavenly Father, and, hopefully, the grace that is extended by brothers and sisters in the faith.

"Failure is not an option" is a famous line attributed to Gene Kranz in the movie *Apollo 13*. In ministry leadership, a more appropriate phrase would be "failure is a certainty." A review of three of the greatest leaders in the Bible (Moses, David, and Peter) reveals that while failure is certain, it is not fatal! The resilient leader learns to embrace the forgiveness and grace of God who is also the one who provides the power to finish well.

SEVEN BARRIERS TO FINISHING WELL[1]

Leaders face many internal challenges which can become critical issues in their ability to continue as effective leaders. Clinton has described what he calls "seven barriers" which keep leaders from finishing well. They are:

1. These "seven barriers" are taken from research by J. Robert Clinton, published in *The Making of a Leader*. The explanations have been added by this author.

1. Finances—The abuse of personal and/or organizational finances can be a challenge which derails many leaders. One particular challenge which can become devastating is the misuse of credit and credit cards. Unhealthy amounts of debt can lead to tremendous personal and relational tension, as well as hinder some ministry opportunities.
2. Power—The desire for power and control, or the misuse of appropriate authority, can quickly lead to the emotional abuse of others. We live in a culture that highly values power. John Stott states, "Still today the three major human ambitions (the pursuit of money, fame, and influence) are all concealed drives for power."[2]
3. Pride—The uncontrolled ego remains an ongoing challenge for leaders throughout their tenures of leadership. This is one of the enemy's greatest tools.
4. Sex—Inappropriate sexual relations, pornography, and lust have destroyed the ministry of many Christian leaders in churches and parachurch organizations. It will remain an ever-present temptation given the sex-saturated society in which we live. These issues (particularly pornography) have been the most prevalent discipline/counseling issues I have faced in my ministries at two different seminaries.
5. Critical Family Issues—This category includes ongoing marital issues, prolonged physical and/or emotional challenges, children with disabilities, and other demanding family concerns. These issues can eventually take a heavy toll on the leader which causes him or her to drop out of leadership.
6. Plateauing—This challenge is one not often recognized by other leaders. It involves living on past knowledge and accomplishments with no ongoing personal and spiritual growth. It is a particular danger for long-term leaders in the same context.

2. Stott, *Basic Christian Leadership*, 36.

7. Emotional Wounding—This challenge refers to unresolved emotional/psychological issues from the past. The wounds most often occurred in the family of origin, but may include other situations as well. Another sensitive time is early adolescence.

Christian leaders are faced with tremendous challenges today. The importance of healthy leadership for churches and other organizations cannot be overstated. It is easy to see why the enemy attacks leaders utilizing every possible avenue of temptation and discouragement. He does not want churches to be healthy and effective. Therefore, if the leaders can be destroyed, the followers will become discouraged and cynical, and the churches will be weak and ineffective.

The seven challenges described above do *not* need to be fatal to a Christian leader! If you have fallen to one of these, it is possible to embrace God's grace and be restored to a role of leadership. But it cannot be done alone. It will require the love, strength, and accountability of other mature leaders. Then, it will be possible to affirm with John Newton:

> I am not what I ought to be, I am not what I want to be, I am not what I hope to be in another world. But still I am not what I once used to be, and by the grace of God I am what I am.

PAUL: SAVED BY GRACE

Paul had a realistic view of who he *was* and who he *is*: "Christ Jesus came into the world to save sinners, of whom I am the foremost. But I received mercy for this reason, that in me, as the foremost, Jesus Christ might display his perfect patience as an example to those who were to believe in him for eternal life" (1 Tim 1:15–16).

Paul also knew that any accomplishments in ministry were through grace and not because he was so good: "But we have this treasure in jars of clay, to show that the surpassing power belongs to God and not to us" (2 Cor 4:7). He continues in the next verses to show that in the midst of persecution, despair, and discouragement, it is God's grace that sustains.

Paul's challenge to his fellow servants is to *embrace grace*! It is this grace that will provide the strength for them to finish well.

Christian leaders can "fail" in many areas: finances, sexuality, misuse of power, and so on. While it is important to build a strong foundation to protect against these failures, if they have occurred, the leader must embrace God's grace.

Paul clearly taught the importance of restoring those who have failed, rather than condemning them: "Brothers, if anyone is caught in any transgression, you who are spiritual should restore him in a spirit of gentleness" (Gal 6:1). One of our responsibilities is to apply grace and not "shoot our wounded."

PETER: EMBRACER OF GRACE

One of the greatest examples of resilient leadership in all of Scripture is the apostle Peter. He was a man of great passion and strong will. Jesus called him as one of the Twelve, and Peter was the first to proclaim that Jesus was the Christ of God. Peter was also the one who denied that he knew Jesus after the arrest in the garden. However, he was restored and became the leader of the early church. By grace, God gave Peter another thirty years of ministry and service.

We need to read and reflect carefully upon the words of this seasoned leader, especially as he drew near to the end of his life. His life and his words serve as an encouragement to us when we have failed or feel like a failure:

> And after you have suffered a little while, the God of all grace, who has called you to his eternal glory in Christ,

> will himself restore, confirm, strengthen, and establish you.[3]

I love Paul David Tripp's comments on this particular verse of scripture:

> If you and I have been guaranteed a place in eternity with our Savior, then we also have been guaranteed all the grace we need along the way. The promise of future grace always carries with it the promise of present grace.[4]

When we fail, let us confess our sins and our errors. With the help of brothers and sisters in Christ, let us embrace the grace which he extends. Let us embrace the forgiveness and healing which he offers. Then, with extra humility and surrender, let us enter again into our leadership roles.

REPAIRING THE PAST

In his excellent book, *A Resilient Life*, Gordon MacDonald has a chapter entitled "Resilient People Understand the Importance of Repairing the Past."[5] The last three sentences in the introductory section leading up to this chapter are a good way to introduce this section:

> Resilient people face the brutal facts of their mistakes, their experiences, their sins, their blessings. And they learn from them. That's how they *repair the past*.[6]

Repairing our past involves an embrace of grace in redemptive and in proactive ways—in redemptive ways as we reflect upon various experiences and events that have shaped us in both positive and negative experiences; in proactive ways as we initiate healing for experiences which were ignored or received no recognition

3. 1 Pet 5:10.
4. Paul David Tripp, *Dangerous Calling*, 223.
5. MacDonald, *A Resilient Life*, 97–104.
6. Ibid., 96.

from others. These two categories are not necessarily exclusive, but may involve some similar dynamics.

Embrace Grace for Past Wrongs

In going through the exercises of the Personal Life Map and the Genogram in chapter eight, it is most likely that you have reflected upon some wrongs that were done to you. Some of these may have been as a result of some leadership activity and others occurred as part of natural life experiences. In some cases, the offending individual may no longer be living. It is important to embrace God's grace and to seek his power to help you forgive. Carrying grudges or hateful feelings will only damage you.

> Forgiveness, I came to see, is about cleaning up the memory by renouncing and flushing vengeful feelings about other people. Forgiveness is about surrendering the right for vengeance and retribution.[7]

In my own times of reflection through the use of these tools, I have had to respond by forgiving others for statements that were made or actions that were taken that wounded me deeply. I continue to seek to embrace God's grace and choose not to carry the hurt and pain. I have learned that forgiveness is both an act and a process.

Embrace Grace for Sins

Most of us identify with Moses, David, Peter, and many other biblical leaders who have failed and sinned against God. I often find myself praying in complete identification with David's shame and guilt which is expressed in Psalm 51.

I have had my share of failures in relationships, within myself, and in leadership experiences. I pray that my heart will be never become hardened against the convicting power of the Holy Spirit.

7. MacDonald, *A Resilient Life*, 128.

When we do sin, we have the privilege of repenting of our sins and seeking God's grace and cleansing (1 John 1:9). Ignoring our sin or trying to excuse our behaviors will only lead to deeper guilt and despair.

One of the biggest challenges is to receive God's grace and forgiveness. We may feel that we are not worthy to continue in leadership. And in some cases, we do need to step out of a public leadership role for a period of time and receive the care and mentoring of a brother, or band of brothers, in the faith. However, as repentance and healing occur, we may know that God will use us again, just as Jesus did with the apostle Peter.

Gordon MacDonald's own story of sin, repentance, sabbatical from public leadership, restoration, and renewal is one of great encouragement. Listen to his statement about the healing value of repentance and restoration:

> Repentance is indispensable to the resilient life. It becomes a habitual spiritual pattern to be practiced regularly. And when a person faces God with an open heart, nothing held back, and what that person relies solely upon the love and grace of Jesus, there is a lightening of the load. The burden is lifted.[8]

I have always loved the quote attributed to Betsy Ten Boom during the days of her imprisonment along with her sister, Corrie, in one of the Nazi concentration camps: "There is no pit so deep that God's love is not deeper still."

This is the message we must embrace when we feel the sting and shame of sin in our lives, thinking that we are in the deepest, darkest pit: God's love *and* God's grace is deeper still!

TODD PARMENTER: LESSONS FROM THE DARK SIDE OF GRACE

I was called to be the Executive Pastor for a church in 2004. It was an exciting time for me, because I had grown up in this

8. MacDonald, *A Resilient Life*, 123.

particular church and attended there until my family moved during my high school years. It was a homecoming that provided the deep sense of satisfaction of serving the church where I met Jesus.

When I arrived, the church had already begun the first phases of a building addition. I took over the helm of that project and saw it to completion. The church was growing, baptism numbers were up, giving was up, people were excited about the ministry, and everything pointed to smooth sailing ahead.

Then the economic collapse of 2008 hit. People were losing their jobs, their retirement accounts were losing over half their value, hours were being cut, and if you were fortunate enough to keep your job, you probably took a pay cut. The offerings began to drop. We made some budget cuts and prayed we would ride it out, but giving continued to decline. We used up our reserve and had decided to cut some part-time staff. I remember the pain of having to let good people go and feeling that I had personally let them down.

Revenue continued to decline. We were unable to pay all the bills. I had to decide between paying the mortgage or paying payroll taxes. Our mortgage was with a local bank, so I chose to not pay the taxes. I also decided *not* to tell the elders, justifying in my mind that we would catch up with the taxes as soon as the revenue turned around. That was in September 2008. I didn't pay the payroll taxes for the remainder of the year. I didn't tell the elders, and I intentionally left it off the financial reports. I kept it from the elders for nine months. When the Department of Revenue began to send notices for the back payroll taxes, I came to my senses and confessed my sin.

I was asked to resign in May 2009; since then, I have been on an exploration to find my true self. Through a week at Blessing Ranch in Colorado, the restoration team, the support of my wife and family, much reading, and a renewed relationship with God, I have come to a deep understanding of who my true self is, and why I am at war with my false self. I would like to talk with you about what I've learned through the process of being a broken-world Christian and *embracing the grace to walk on the path of restoration*.

I have found that growing up in the church, I had begun to live in a false self that was motivated more from a theology of works than a theology of grace. I had begun to wear this mask that everything was okay and that I could handle anything that came my way. I stuffed my fear of failure deep down inside and projected that I was capable, committed to the church, and a good person. Although these things are not bad in themselves, when you live that way you depend on your own ability. When I succeed, I am good. When I fail, I am bad and no longer capable. Without the grace from God to fail, failure to perform brings judgment instead of grace. This internalization of a theology of works creates an environment that is ripe for a broken-world experience. I have come to call this the dark side of grace.

There are several motivations that can move a person into a practice of a theology of works. The one that is most often discussed is the personality trait of being a people-pleaser. A people-pleaser is someone who cannot say "no" and who over-extends themselves in order to please others. Although it does not garner as much discussion, I believe there is a motivation towards a theology of works that is greater than the people-pleaser. It is dangerously destructive. It destroys relationships and drives people from the church in droves, vowing never to return. It is a theology of works as compensation for the unconfessed sin in our lives.

If you study the Scriptures, you find that the early church made confession and forgiveness a priority for the life of the church. Confession and forgiveness was not done privately, it was done in community. I believe that is what is needed to reclaim the theology of grace in the New Testament church.

I greatly appreciated that my restoration team and my church recognized the role and value of public confession of sin. In a public service, I confessed my sin and asked for forgiveness. And the leaders publicly accepted my confession and my repentance. I have learned that my Lord Jesus loves me whether in a state of grace or disgrace!

A STORY OF GRACE AND RESILIENCE[9]

In 1986, the United Methodist Council of Bishops sent American Bishop David Lawson to Liberia at the height of the Liberian civil war. Bishop Lawson's job was to help keep his Liberian colleague, Bishop Arthur Kulah, out of jail. Lawson also was asked to visit other Liberian pastors who had been incarcerated and to seek their freedom. "That's all that was asked of me," Bishop Lawson remarks with a wry smile.

The second day he was there, Bishop Kulah's assistant invited Lawson on a three-and-a-half-hour drive outside the city. When they arrived, Bishop Lawson followed his guide up a hill to a patch of ground where a square plot was formed by evergreens. In the middle of the plot was a small, square, concrete box. There was nothing ornate about the unmarked box. No inscriptions, nothing to indicate what it was.

The bishop stood silently beside his host, who quietly wept while looking at the box. Finally Bishop Lawson broke the silence and gently asked what they were looking at.

"You don't know the story?" his host asked. "This is a story of the Fadleys, a young couple who were American seminary graduates and missionaries to Liberia. He was an agriculturalist, sent to teach Liberians how to grow crops from this arid land. She was a teacher who started schools in many of the surrounding territories. The people here fell in love with the Fadleys, and they fell in love with the Liberians."

Eventually, the wife began to fall weak. The doctors couldn't find what was wrong with her and suggested that they return to the States for a better examination. But the Fadleys lingered. There

9. Quoted directly from Jones and Armstrong, *Resurrecting Excellence*, 175–176.

were crops to plant, schools to start, congregations that were arising from their work. This was home.

Mrs. Fadley eventually became so weak that she couldn't travel even if she wanted to. At the end of her life, she asked her husband for one last favor. "We've loved these people," she said. "What we've been doing is beautiful and important. Our hearts belong here. When I die you can ship my body home. My parents would want that. But first I want you to ask the surgeons to remove my heart. I want my heart here."

At that moment, Bishop Lawson knew what was in the box. "I knew I was on holy ground. I stood there silently beside this weeping assistant, and all I could think about was whether there was any group, any place, any people in this world that I should regard as so important and beautiful that I would want to bury my heart in that place, with those people."

> May our God grant us the grace and resilience to finish so well!!

APPENDIX ONE

Biblical Foundations for Mentoring

Old Testament Models	New Testament Models
Jethro and Moses (Exod 18)	Jesus and the 12 (Mark 3:13–14)
Moses and Joshua (Deut 31)	Barnabas and Saul (Acts)
Jonathan and David (1 Sam 18–20)	Priscilla & Aquilla and Apollos (Acts)
Elijah and Elisha (1 Kgs 19; 2 Kgs 2–3)	Paul and Timothy (Acts 16; 1, 2 Tim)
Jehoida and Joash (2 Chr 24)	Paul and Titus (2 Cor 7; Titus)

Although the word "mentor" does not appear in the New Testament, there are many words or images associated with mentoring. The primary words are:

1. Disciple (mathetes)—appears 261 times in the gospels and Acts
2. To disciple (matheteuo)—appears only 4 times
3. To learn (manthano)—appears 52 times
4. To follow (akoloutheo)—appears 90 times
5. To imitate (mimeomai) or imitator (mimetes)—appear 11 times

For use of these words or concepts, the following passages provide examples:

Mark 3:14	2 Thessalonians 3:9
Luke 6:40	1 Timothy 4:12
1 Corinthians 4:16; 11:1	2 Timothy 3:10
Philippians 3:17; 4:9	Titus 2:7–8
1 Thessalonians 1:6–8	Hebrews 13:7

Key Text: ". . .what you have heard from me in the presence of many witnesses entrust to faithful men who will be able to teach others also." (2 Tim 2:2)

APPENDIX TWO

Examples of a Personal Philosophy of Ministry

EXAMPLE ONE

- **Christ is the head of the church and its leader (Eph 1:22–23, 4:15–16, 5:23–24; Col 2:19).** Without submitting to the lordship of Christ and the truth of Scripture, any effort to build a church community and do ministry in the name of Christianity is in vain. Christ's example of submission and obedience to the Father is the reason why leadership must obediently submit to him. As the sovereign ruler, he is the one who gives authority to others, in order that they might be instruments of his character and promoting his kingdom. A leader who submits to Christ's leadership must daily choose to listen for his voice and direction, living a life of prayer, devotion, and obedience to Scripture.
- **The church exists for the mission of God (Gen 12:3; Isa 60:1–4; Matt 5:13–16, 28:18–20).** Ministry in the church operates with the desire to do all things to the glory of God and to make his name known among the nations. Without a desire to see others come into fellowship with Christ and believers living in surrendered obedience, ministry is not

fulfilling its purpose or intention. This means that although members within the church—including its leaders—will sin and not always reflect the mission of Christ, God's plan and purpose in using people to spread his gospel has not failed. Ministry seeks to honestly critique and praise the work of the church, without excusing weaknesses or worshipping it as an institution.

- **Pastors and leaders in the church are shepherds and disciple-makers (Ezek 34; John 10; Acts 2:42–47; 1 Pet 5:1–11).** Following the example of Christ, who loved the church and gave himself up for her, leadership involves the cost of denying self and selfish ambition. A good shepherd knows the needs, weaknesses, and strengths of the sheep and functions as a leader who teaches, corrects, feeds, and cares for those under his or her care. Ministry must be lived out in the day-to-day, real-life situations of people, and it is through intentional relationships and mentoring that leaders disciple others. A ministry that exists without a culture of discipleship—a culture where each member understands the importance of learning in community and teaching the next generation—does not fulfill the organic, rhythmic intention of the Great Commission and the call to protect the church from false doctrine.
- **Every believer is called to ministry (Acts 2:42; Rom 12:3–8; 1 Cor 12; Eph 4:7–16; 1 Pet 2:9–10).** While pastors and leaders in the church may be tempted to see their work as higher callings than those of "the laity," Scripture teaches that ministry is a communal effort, with each function empowered by the Spirit. Every believer has the joy and responsibility of sharing in the work of the church and proclaiming the gospel, without making distinctions between sacred and secular vocations. Pastors and leaders should model this conviction by allowing others to exercise their various gifts within the community, expanding the ministry and spiritual growth of the church.

Personal Giftedness

Based on the DISC profile, my blended profiles reflect the role of a supporter and a performer. This blend of traits allows me seek excellence in every area of ministry and find ways to encourage and motivate others to grow and use their gifts within the church. I thrive on relating to others and finding creative ways to teach the gospel so that the community of faith can be strengthened. I desire to use the experiences and training the Lord has provided me with to teach students in higher education who want to be pastors, educators, and leaders within the Christian community. I also desire to serve on a pastoral team within a local church, focusing on strengthening its teaching and community life.

Biblical Core Values

- **Holistic—Ministry involves every area of life.** Leaders not only offer their gifts and abilities, but time, prayer support, and resources to every individual. Ministry and the Christian life is not segmented, but integrated.
- **Creativity—Ministry allows a variety of methods and mediums to communicate the gospel.** As those created in the image of God, all people are given the ability to create and share their giftedness with others; this includes the ways ministry seeks to communicate the Gospel, without altering its timeless, truthful message.
- **Community—Genuine, authentic relationships are a sign of a healthy ministry.** Leaders are not defined by how many people are under their care, but on how they understand the needs and joys of the household of faith. Ministry is not done alone, but as a community of believers.
- **Cooperation—The mission of God and service to others can and should be done by partnering with other groups of Christ-followers.** The Church is not defined by a local church's denomination, size, or geographical location, but

allows those factors to influence and assist others by combining resources, talents, and differences.

- **Submission—Ministry submits to the Word, example of Christ, and leadership of the Spirit.** It is this dependence on the Word and surrender to the Spirit that enables leaders to lead in humility and empower others in the church to lead alongside them.
- **Sacrifice—Ministry seeks to build the name of Christ, not build the name of an individual, community, strategy, or denomination.** Leaders follow the sacrificial example of Christ, who taught that following him requires taking up the cross and dying to self daily.
- **Perseverance—Ministry does not give up.** All believers are called to remain faithful and committed to following Christ, regardless of the cost and discomfort it brings.
- **Growth—A leader never "arrives" in ministry, but continues to grow in a teachable spirit.** Scripture continues to change and shape the heart, allowing the leader to continue to conform more to the image of Christ. Culture and communities change, encouraging the leader to continue to engage in current, meaningful dialogue with others.
- **Authority—Christ is the ultimate authority, and the Holy Spirit is responsible for empowering ministry.** A leader cannot operate from a CEO or hierarchical perspective, but must recognize that the same Spirit dwells within each member of the body of Christ.

EXAMPLE TWO

- **The Church is God's chosen instrument (Gen 12:3; Eph 3:21; Matt 28:19; Acts 1:8).** The church is a unique spiritual organization chosen by God in order to glorify him. To that end, the Church builds itself up in the faith through the instruction in the word, through fellowship with one another, through the keeping of the ordinances, and by advancing and communicating the gospel of Jesus Christ throughout the world. The church is not perfect; its members and its leaders will continue to sin. However, just because this is the case does not mean that God's plan and purpose for the church has failed.

- **Christ is head of the church (Eph 1:22–23; 4:15–16; Col 1:18; 2:19).** The one supreme authority for the Church is Jesus Christ. To the extent that the Church submits itself to the lordship of Christ and to the truth of Scripture, effective ministry and growth of the body will occur. It is the need of the Church to cooperate with God, under the lordship of Christ, as God accomplishes his purposes in the Church and in the world. To that end, spiritual gifts are given to each member of the body that enable it to accomplish God's purposes.
- **Pastors are shepherds, equippers, and disciple makers (Eph 4:11–12; Rev 22:12; John 21:15–19).** Pastors are to follow the example of Christ and serve as under-shepherds of the people of God. To that end, they must imitate Christ's love for the church and his self-sacrificial attitude and actions for the church. Ministry among the body must be done through personal relationships. On a macro-level, the pastor shepherds and equips the entire body through the preaching of the word and through overall direction and guidance of the church. On a micro-level, the pastor must identify a smaller group of professional and lay leaders that he disciples and mentors with the intention that they do the same for others. The pastor should also identify means and methods of developing and maintaining relationships with the lost in order to make them disciples of Jesus Christ.
- **Every believer is called to ministry (Eph 4:12–13; 1 Cor 3:12–13; 2 Pet 2:4–5).** Ministry is a communal effort on behalf of the entire church. Every believer in Jesus Christ is called into the "royal priesthood." While the church may be tempted to see their pastor as a surrogate through which they

minister, Scripture teaches that every believer has the joy and responsibility of sharing in the work of the Church and proclaiming the gospel, without distinction between sacred and secular vocations.

- **The Holy Spirit empowers the church in ministry (Rom 8:9–11; 1 Cor 12:1–11; 1 Cor 3:6).** The Holy Spirit is the supernatural and sovereign agent in regeneration and baptizes all believers into the body of Christ. Subsequently, he indwells, sanctifies, instructs, and empowers each believer for service. The Church must avoid attempts to be empowered by other sources such as entertainment, or marketing, or church growth strategies and earnestly seek to be a Spirit-empowered body. The Church can only accomplish its goal of glorifying God under the direction of Jesus Christ if the Holy Spirit gives it the power.

Giftedness

Based on my DISC profile, the strengths identified through the Clifton Strengths Finder, and personal experience, my giftedness lies in the area of preaching and teaching. I have an intense hunger and thirst for the Word of God and a driving passion to preach and teach it to others. I thrive on understanding the Bible and my congregation and helping them see how the Bible, and through it, Christ, provides all the strength and equipping that they need in order to faithfully follow him and exercise their own spiritual gifts within the church, their local community, and the world. To that end, I desire to use these gifts in a lead pastor role within a local congregation that focuses on personal and corporate growth in Christlikeness, growth in our connectedness to one another, and growth of the church through living out the Great Commission.

Core Values

- **Christlikeness—The foundation of ministry is character.** The minister must first be Christlike before he can lead others to be Christlike. Effective ministry will flow out of who the minister is.
- **Connectedness—Authentic relationships are the true sign of a healthy church.** The health of the church is not defined by numbers. It is defined by how Christlike the congregation is and how connected by genuine, authentic, Christ-honoring relationships exist.
- **Commission—The Church's one goal is to make disciples.** Disciple-making is a holistic activity that encompasses ministry to children, youth, and adults within the church as well as evangelism outside of the church.
- **Service—Christian leadership is leading through service.** The Church's calling is to serve one another like Christ served his disciples and the people he came into contact with. It is the minister's responsibility to model this to the congregation.
- **Sacrifice—Ministry is about glorifying God and building the church of Jesus Christ.** It is not about the minister or his glory. He must continue to die to himself every day as he continues to serve Christ and the church. He is a servant and does what his master commands him even when he doesn't feel like it or when it runs contrary to his own circumstances. He will sacrifice to serve Christ.
- **Simplicity—Ministers best serve when their cup overflows.** The minister must guard his time carefully to avoid so much service that he becomes burned out. The minister should have sufficient time for personal study of Scripture, prayer and meditation on the Word, and family life. Quality and effectiveness of ministry will increase or decrease in proportion to this time.

- **Submission—Ministers who willingly submit to the Lordship of Christ will more properly exercise authority over others.** A minister must first learn submission to Christ before he can lead others to do the same and before he can appropriately exercise any authority over the congregation.
- **Unity—The Church should reflect a unified purpose.** The pastor should lead in such a way as to foster unity of purpose even if diversity of method is present. To that end, the pastor should be a consensus builder around Biblical means and methods of accomplishing that purpose.
- **Perseverance—Ministry does not give up.** Believers are called to persevere in their salvation and in their service. Anything else brings reproach upon the name of Christ and the minster.

APPENDIX THREE

DiSC Overview

ACTIVE STYLES

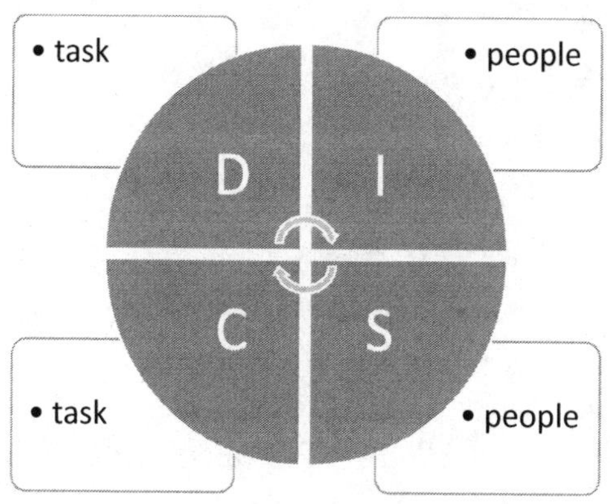

PASSIVE STYLES

D	I	S	C
•forceful	•optimistic	•steady	•precise
•direct	•friendly	•patient	•sensitive
•strong-willed	•talkative	•loyal	•analytical
•impatient	•charismatic	•practical	•idealistic

APPENDIX FOUR
Maintaining Balance

(Mark 12:29–30)

1. Physical Self-leadership
   - Diet and nutrition:
     - Key is balance and moderation
     - Eat more whole-grains, vegetables, fruits, & lower fat proteins
     - Avoid foods high in saturated fat or sugar
     - Drink 6–10 glasses of water daily
   - Occasional fasting (skipping 1–2 meals)
   - Consistent exercise program
     - Balance of: cardiovascular, strength, and flexibility
     - Minimum of 30 minutes 4–6 times per week
     - Mental benefits
     - Weight benefits
   - Medical care—appropriate check-ups & prevention
     - Appropriate rest and relaxation
2. Emotional Self-leadership

- Personal motivation
- Regulation of emotions (e.g., anger, worry, depression)
- Social interactions

3. Mental/intellectual Self-leadership
    - Systematic study and/or educational program
    - Recreational reading
    - Involvement in the arts
    - Teaching or leading others

4. Spiritual Self-leadership
    - Personal retreats (meditation, prayer)
    - Reading spiritual materials (e.g., Bible)
    - Journaling

APPENDIX FIVE

Personal Life Map

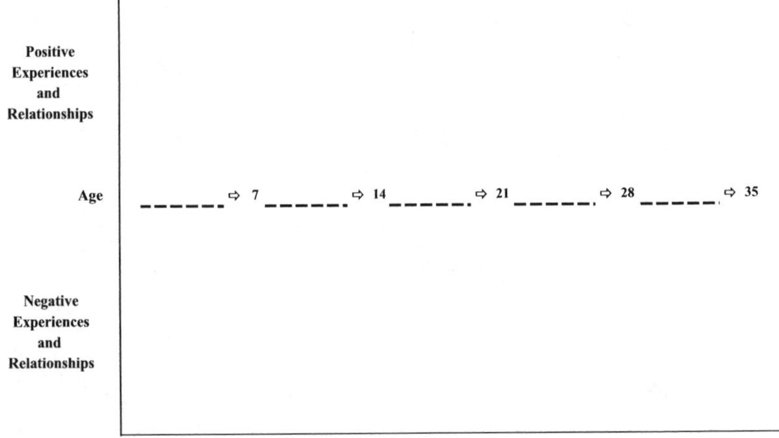

APPENDIX SIX

Heart-Shaping Factors

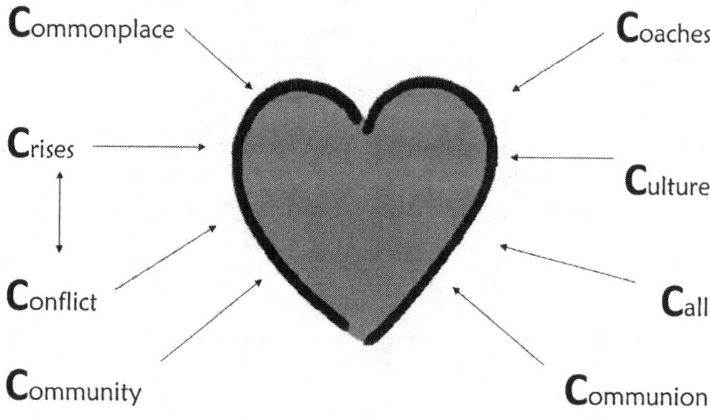

APPENDIX SEVEN

Johari Window for Self-Understanding

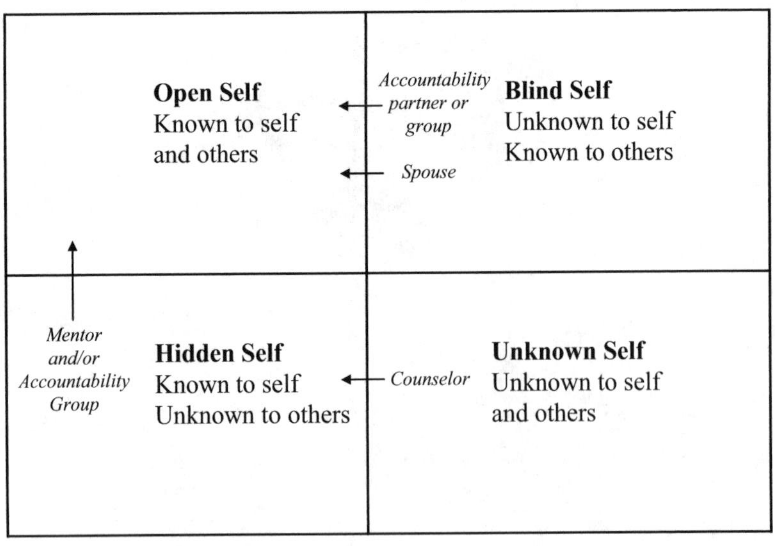

Dr. Mark Searby
Beeson Divinity School

APPENDIX EIGHT

Genograms Article

UTILIZING GENOGRAMS TO DEVELOP SELF-AWARENESS AND REFLECTION SKILLS WITH BEGINNING DMIN STUDENTS*

Mark A. Searby, DMin
Director of Doctor of Ministry Studies
Beeson Divinity School, Samford University
Birmingham, Alabama

Susan Goble, MS
Adjunct Instructor, Beeson Divinity School
Licensed Marriage and Family Therapist

***The following pages are drawn from the full paper designated above and was originally presented at the ADME (Association of Doctor of Ministry Education) Conference in New Orleans in 2012. The full paper is available from the author.**

THEORETICAL BASE FOR GENOGRAMS

Leaders are not shaped in isolation. Leaders are shaped *in* community. And they are shaped *by* community.

> Leaders cannot be separated from the formative processes of community.[1]

> It is clear that our family experience during our young, dependent years shapes and sculpts who we become to a considerable degree. While many of the details of this are known, there is much still to be learned.[2]

Each person is unique, having been shaped by a combination of nature, nurture, and life experiences. Undoubtedly, one's family of origin is the most significant shaping community he or she experiences.

An important place to begin in understanding our family of origin and our place in that family is to create a genogram. A genogram (also called a "family diagram" by some authors) is a diagrammatic method for depicting multiple generations of one's family of origin for the purpose of gaining a better understanding of emotional processes which have shaped the individual.

A genogram is not the same as a family tree. The genogram is an outgrowth of family systems theory. It reflects the emotional processes through the generations and is only useful as the principles of family systems theory are applied. It provides a tool for deeper reflection and discussion for the individual.

Below is an example of a genogram:

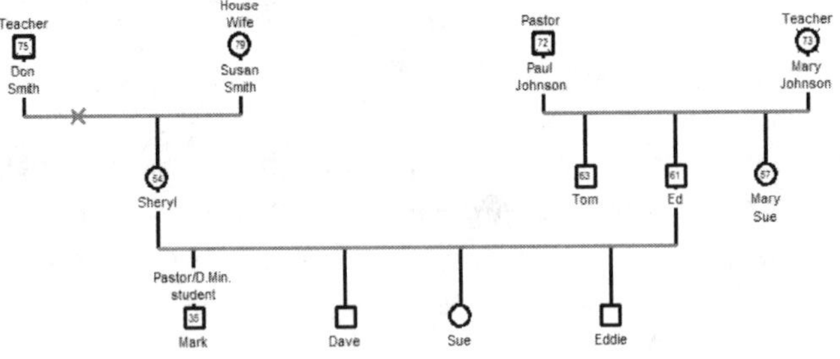

1. McNeal, *A Work of Heart*, 115.
2. Gilbert, *Extraordinary Leadership*, 33.

The genogram above is a three-generation diagram. The three-generation diagram is utilized in the Beeson program and will be detailed in the next section.

While it is not the intention of this paper to explain the theory undergirding the genogram at length, it is important to understand some of the key concepts which are involved in this theory. The following concepts will be described briefly: differentiation of self, fusion, emotional triangles, anxiety, and family projections.

Emotional maturity and emotionally mature behaviors are goals of understanding ourselves within our current systems. "This is expressed through emotional separation from our parents and is described as differentiation of self, the capacity to offer a thoughtful response rather than react emotionally, the ability to remain connected to important people in our lives without having our behavior and reactions determined by them."[3]

Differentiation of self is the ability to define oneself based upon a set of guiding principles. It includes the ability to take responsibility for one's own emotions, to allow others to be themselves, and the ability to maintain a less-anxious presence in the midst of chaos or highly anxious situations while remaining connected to others within healthy relationship boundaries.

Fusion refers to excessive unresolved emotional attachments that were developed through years of experience in one's family of origin. "They derive from the family anxiety and focus that resulted in an excessive emotional attachment; first to parents, then to other important relationships."[4]

Emotional triangles are neither good nor bad. They are a fact of life in human relationships, in families and in organizations. However, whenever there is a high level of anxiety in relationships, individuals begin to talk *about* each other rather than *to* each other. Highly involved triangles devolve into gossip and rumor spreading.

3. Herrington, Creech, and Taylor, *The Leader's Journey*, 34. This book is utilized as a text for the initial seminar for new DMin students at Beeson.

4. Gilbert, *Extraordinary Leadership*, 69.

Anxiety refers to intense emotion of most any type. Gilbert offers the definition of "heightened reactivity."[5] Families and organizations are subject to acute and chronic anxiety. Acute reactions occur whenever there is a real threat. Chronic anxiety is the result of an imagined or distorted threat. These threats may occur from within the system or from outside the system.

Family projections refers to the process in which anxiety within a family is projected onto one particular member of the family unit. It may result in a great deal of focus being placed upon a child in a positive or negative manner. This may lead to a higher level of fusion within the family and potentially to more immaturity for the individual and the family.

It is important to utilize these key concepts in processing one's own genogram. For instance, one might ask: "What were the levels of fusion in my family of origin with my parents and siblings?" or "How was anxiety handled in my family and extended family?"

Another useful concept for students to utilize in this process is the understanding of "functional positions" which are given typically in most families. Gilbert provides the following list of positions with a brief explanation of each:

1. The "good one"
2. The "rebel"
3. The "sick one"
4. The "caretaker"
5. The "family therapist"
6. The "star"
7. The "comic"
8. The "favored child"[6]

The insights gained from a new understanding of self within one's family of origin help the student grow in his relationships with the nuclear family and in the congregational family. Since the

5. Ibid., 187.
6. Gilbert, *Extraordinary Leadership*, 38–42.

emotional experience of our family of origin has had an impact upon how we perceive ourselves, our relationships with others, and our decision-making process, there will be a cumulative impact upon our own nuclear family as well as our ministry context (system) as we make these new connections.

Learning to think and reflect from a systems perspective is an important step in becoming a more mature individual and effective leader.

> Once we see how we are all a part of a larger unit—the family—and that the patterns or postures are not good or bad, but rather simply a part of the human phenomenon, we can begin to observe more calmly, letting go of blame, censure, and hostility. We stop making diagnoses and trying to figure out who is at fault. Observation is key to understanding what is happening in the system and managing oneself well in it. The observing thinking leader becomes curious, engaged, and open to new learning.[7]

SOURCES AND RESOURCES

Benner, David G. *The Gift of Being Yourself.* Downers Grove, IL: InterVarsity, 2004.

Friedman, Edwin H. *Generation to Generation.* New York: Guilford, 1985.

Gilbert, Roberta M. *Extraordinary Leadership: Thinking Systems, Making a Difference.* Falls Church, VA: Leading Systems Press, 2006.

Herrington, Jim, R. Robert Creech, and Trisha Taylor. *The Leader's Journey: Accepting the Call to Personal and Congregational Transformation.* San Francisco: Jossey-Bass, 2003.

Kerr, Michael E., and Murray Bowen. *Family Evaluation.* New York: Norton, 1988.

McGoldrick, Monica, Randy Gerson, and Sylvia Shellenberger. *Genograms: Assessment and Intervention.* New York: Norton, 1999.

McNeal, Reggie. *A Work of Heart.* San Francisco: Jossey-Bass, 2000.

Richardson, Ronald W. *Becoming a Healthier Pastor: Family Systems Theory and the Pastor's Own Family.* Minneapolis: Fortress, 2005.

Steinke, Peter L. *How Your Church Family Works: Understanding Congregations as Emotional Systems.* Herndon, VA: The Alban Institute, 2006.

7. Ibid., 16.

APPENDIX NINE
Genogram Questions

1. Describe each family member with three adjectives and their relationship.
2. Describe your parents' relationship.
3. How was conflict handled in your family?
4. How were gender roles and authority worked out in your family?
5. How well did your family do in talking about feelings?
6. How would your family describe you?
7. How was sexuality talked or not talked about? What were the implied messages?
8. Were there any family "secrets"?
9. What was considered "success" in your family?
10. How was money handled?
11. How did your family's ethnicity shape you?
12. Were there any heroes or heroines in the family? Scapegoats? Losers?
13. What kinds of addictions, if any, existed in your family?
14. Were there traumatic losses in the past or present, such as sudden death, bankruptcy, etc.?

15. How was spirituality expressed?

From *The Emotionally Healthy Church* by Peter Scazzero

APPENDIX TEN

"Why Leaders Blow Up" —Paper by John Walker

John Walker, PhD
Blessing Ranch Ministries
New Port Richey, Florida

WHY LEADERS BLOW UP: SIGNS OF A SERIOUS WRECK WAITING TO HAPPEN

"What to watch for to avoid crashing and burning"

We have all heard of "serious wrecks" within leadership ministry. The stories are all too familiar. Too often we hear "I never saw it coming." Therefore, the following are intended to increase awareness that a "serious wreck" may be imminent so that it might be avoided.

Generic Signs: The Five General Risk Factors

- Running on empty (chronic over-expenditure of personal resources with limited replenishment)
- Isolationism and relational stress (interpersonal withdrawal with irritability and critical behavior)

- Dark clouds (generalized sense of discouragement, despair, and defeat)
- Serious hurts internalized (hurts minimized and rationalized on the exterior, yet harbored on the interior)
- Self-reliance (a pervasive sense that "I can handle this" on my own)

Pretenders have significant "success" but believe they are impostors who are in way over their heads. Their fear is that others will discover their inadequacy and/or incompetency. They refuse to face themselves. Therefore, watch for:

- Workaholism to prove significance and cover inadequacies. Worth via performance.
- Contempt for inefficiency and ineffectiveness.
- An inability to be transparent and real with others. Watch for pseudo-transperancy.
- Interpersonal distance to keep others from being able to fully know them. Watch for pseudo-intimacy.
- A self-image formed via experience instead of the Word of God.
- Inability to accept a compliment because it is inconsistent with private logic.
- Brief episodes of unexpected or out of the blue emotionality.

A decompensated (serious wreck) pretender is completely overwhelmed and humiliated. They give up, believing that there is no longer any hope. They are demoralized and immobilized into complete ineffectiveness and withdrawal. They want to run away.

Procrastinators over-rely on their cognitive abilities as a means of avoiding affect. An out of awareness fear is that feelings will be overwhelming. Consequently, logic is exclusively valued over feelings. Feelings are often seen as a sign of weakness. Much is out of their awareness. They refuse to face their feelings. Therefore, watch for:

- "Mr. Spock" persona with over-controlled emotions.
- A cyclic pattern over time of outstanding performance with brief periods of depression and defeatism (temporary loss of perspective).
- Little insight into their own psychological functioning. Little self-awareness.
- Hidden sin patterns to self-medicate repressed affect.
- Limited capacity for compassion and empathy, unless the other is judged to be a "basket case."
- Periodically offends others, but "doesn't get it."
- Limited capacity to intuit feelings in others.

A decompensated (serious wreck) procrastinator often experiences overwhelming affect with no ability to manage it. Every internalized fear is realized, and they cannot cope. Sometimes they do something "really stupid." Others experience a crisis of faith. Their world falls apart.

Paralytics evolve into "not being themselves." There is often a marked change in behavior, thought, and spirit. The power of a secret has controlled them. They compartmentalize incongruencies between their spiritual beliefs and their behaviors. They only have a limited awareness of the incongruity, and it tends to grow with time. Their fear is that they are "in too deep" to come clean and believe that cover-up is their only means of coping. They refuse to face their sin. Therefore, watch for:

- Sneakiness and slipperiness via evasive words.
- Unaccountable time. There is often "offense" when confronted as a means of covering up.
- Pseudo-accountability.
- Loss of confidence in self, God, and others.

- A growing sense of irritability and ineffectiveness.
- Self-reliance with a mix of shame and guilt.

A decompensated (serious wreck) paralytic often experiences debilitating spiritual, emotional, and physical effects. Having given up emotionally and spiritually, they sometimes behave outrageously, showing little self-control, believing they are completely rejected so why bother to try. Other paralytics crash into utter despair, depression, hopelessness, and helplessness.

HOW TO AVOID A SERIOUS WRECK OR ASSIST WITH ONE THAT'S ALREADY HAPPENED

(Helping emotional pretenders, procrastinators, and paralytics)

Pretenders have at their core a self-image of inadequacy even though there is significant evidence of achievement. The problem is that their successes don't really heal the hole in their souls. Pretenders are best helped through insight via a "competent other."

- Insight into themselves needs to focus on rearranging the self-image.
- Self-image must move from worth through achievement to a self-concept formed "via the eyes of God."
- Explore their private logic, especially around how their family of origin valued or didn't value them.
- Pretenders need deep collegial relationships where they can risk being real.
- Theologically, pretenders need a personal grace encounter.

Procrastinators over rely on their cognitive abilities to the point of ignoring the affect that is very present in their lives. They must learn to integrate awareness of affect into their world of cognition. They learn best through guided discovery with a "safe other."

- Regularly ask procrastinators how they are feeling as a means of increasing awareness. Do not let them get away with answering that question with a "thought."
- Help them to label feelings that they do not understand in themselves and others.
- Within a very safe relationship, give regular feedback about how you see them functioning, especially on an emotional level.
- Help them learn the value of personal ongoing rest and renewal.
- Insist on personal accountability and watch for hidden sin patterns that self-medicate repressed feelings.
- Theologically, they need to understand their relationship with God on a feeling level.

Paralytics rarely expose their inner self because they have something to hide. They are excellent at deflecting others as a means of facilitating their "cover-up strategy." They learn best through a "caring other" who will strongly confront.

- Paralytics need strong confrontation but within the context of care, support, and acceptance. Yet be aware that they will be strongly defended and very convincing when confronted with the truth.
- They need significant healing for inner shame.
- They often need significant encouragement to increase confidence.
- They must learn strategies to approach problems rather than avoid them.
- Theologically, they need repentance and increased sensitivity to the role of convictions in their lives via the Holy Spirit. Often they need to differentiate between "neurotic guilt" and "conviction of God."

PAIN, PERSPECTIVE, AND PROCESS: JEREMIAH, THE PROPHET

Jeremiah provides hope for pretenders, procrastinators, and paralytics. If we are honest, there is some of each in all of us. What Jeremiah faced in ministry is not dissimilar to what we face today. While he was a prophet of encouragement, he was also a prophet of despair. Most of his ministry seemed to be "rowing up-current." Sometimes he had to wonder if he could really survive his ministry. His audience was unresponsive and even indicated that his message was not from God. "Results" were absent. He knew deep despair as if he was "doomed to ministry." Yet he knew that if he did not speak the word of the Lord, it would be a fire in his bones. In spite of—or maybe even because of—all this, he is a mighty prophet of God. So, what's up with that?

1. He learned that crisis time is good news. He learned this perspective through a process of experiencing God's sufficiency and teaching in times of personal suffering and tragedy. Suffering often gives us the opportunity to do something different, but we must face our imperfections and weakness.
2. He learned to face his pain. Facing imperfection often causes pain. When it does or looks like it will, many of us do not have the emotional or spiritual maturity to face the pain. Instead, our fears or faulty private logic leads us to run from or cover the pain in a way that does not lead to growth.
3. He learned to see pain as instructive. Many times, God is the author of our pain. Too many times we see pain as the enemy and believe that it is from Satan. Our attributions suggest that our lives and ministries would be better if painful circumstances and people were out of our lives. If we misattribute our pain, or if we resist looking at our pain, we often resist the blessings of God. We also resist getting beyond ourselves, our feelings, and our sin.
4. He experienced significant emotional and spiritual growth. Seeing the big picture, gaining understanding, and learning

via the perspective of God leads to growth. Growth and blessing often come through pain. Look at the progression of our Lord. Gethsemane required Jesus to face the conflicting wills of self and God. He finds the courage to face the fear of Golgotha. At Golgotha he enters into the pain. Glory follows.

Too many times, pretenders, procrastinators, and paralytics get stuck and stay stuck because they have difficulty recognizing the signs and fear facing the issues. In addition, they chronically mislabel problems and consequently apply incorrect and inadequate solutions. This impairs growth as a prophet.

The process of blending emotional and spiritual growth for significant Christian leaders often involves intentional collegiality that gives perspective, challenges, finds creative solutions, and "walks in the soul" of the other along the path of God.

BIBLIOGRAPHY

Allain-Chapman, Justine. *Resilient Pastors.* London: SPCK, 2012

Allender, Dan B. *Leading With a Limp.* Colorado Springs, CO: WaterBrook, 2006.

Anderson, Keith R., and Randy D. Reese. *Spiritual Mentoring.* Downers Grove, IL: InterVarsity, 1999.

Benner, David G. *The Gift of Being Yourself.* Downers Grove, IL: InterVarsity, 2004.

Blanchard, Ken, and Phil Hodges. *The Servant Leader.* Nashville: Thomas Nelson, 2003.

Boa, Kenneth. *Conformed to His Image.* Grand Rapids, MI: Zondervan, 2001.

Brain, Peter. *Going the Distance.* Kingsford, Australia: Matthias Media, 2006.

Brown, Colin, ed. "Patience." In *Dictionary of New Testament Theology, Vol.* 2, 764–76. Grand Rapids, MI: Zondervan, 1976.

Buckingham, Marcus, and Donald O. Clifton. *Now, Discover Your Strengths.* New York: The Free Press, 2001.

Burns, Bob, Tasha D. Chapman, and Donald C. Guthrie. *Resilient Ministry.* Downers Grove, IL: IVP Books, 2013.

Calhoun, Adele Ahlberg. *Spiritual Disciplines Handbook.* Downers Grove, IL: IVP Books, 2005.

Calvin, John. *Institutes of the Christian Religion.* Translated by Henry Beveridge. Grand Rapids, MI: Eerdmans, 1981.

Carroll, Jackson W. *God's Potters: Pastoral Leadership and the Shaping of Congregations.* Grand Rapids, MI: Eerdmans, 2006.

Clinton, J. Robert. *The Making of a Leader.* Colorado Springs, CO: NavPress, 1988.

Cloud, Henry, and John Townsend. *Boundaries.* Grand Rapids, MI: Zondervan, 1992.

Cole, Neil. *Journeys to Significance.* San Francisco: Jossey-Bass, 2011.

Coleman, Robert E. *The Master Plan of Evangelism.* Grand Rapids, MI: Revell, 1963.

Collins, Gary R. *Christian Coaching.* Colorado Springs, CO: NavPress, 2009.

Cordeiro, Wayne. *Leading on Empty.* Minneapolis, MN: Bethany House, 2009.

Bibliography

Cousins, Don. *Experiencing LeaderShift: Letting Go of Leadership Heresies*. Colorado Springs, CO: David C. Cook, 2008.

Covey, Stephen R. *The 7 Habits of Highly Effective People*. New York: Fireside, 1989.

Foster, Richard. *Celebration of Discipline*. San Francisco: Harper & Row, 1978.

Fuller Institute of Church Growth. "1991 Survey of Pastors." Pasadena, CA: Fuller Theological Seminary, 1991.

Gilbert, Roberta M. *Extraordinary Leadership: Thinking Systems, Making a Difference*. Falls Church, VA: Leading Systems Press, 2006.

Harney, Kevin. *Leadership from the Inside Out*. Grand Rapids, MI: Zondervan, 2007.

Heifetz, Ronald A., and Marty Linsky. *Leadership on the Line*. Boston: Harvard Business School Press, 2002.

Herrington, Jim, R. Robert Creech, and Trisha Taylor. *The Leader's Journey*. San Francisco: Jossey-Bass, 2003.

Heuser, Roger, and Norman Shawchuck. *Leading the Congregation*. Nashville: Abingdon, 2010.

Howell, Don N. *Servants of the Servant*. Eugene, OR: Wipf & Stock, 2003.

Hudson, Trevor. *Discovering Our Spiritual Identity*. Downers Grove, IL: IVP Books, 2010.

Inscape Publishing. *A Comparison of DiSC®Classic and the Myers-Briggs Type Indicator® Research Report*. Minneapolis, MN: Inscape Publishing, 1996.

Johnson, W. Brad, and Charles R. Ridley. *The Elements of Mentoring*. New York: Palgrave Macmillan, 2008.

Jones, L. Gregory, and Kevin R. Armstrong. *Resurrecting Excellence*. Grand Rapids, MI: Eerdmans, 2006.

Kram, Kathy. *Mentoring at Work*. Lanham, MD: University Press of America, 1988.

Kulp, Andrew P. *Gifted2Serve, Finding Your Place in Ministry: An Online Spiritual Gifts Inventory*. Auburn, AL: Building Church Ministries, 2001. www.buildingchurch.net/g2s

London, H. B., and Neil B. Wiseman. *Pastors at Greater Risk*. Ventura, CA: Regal, 2003.

MacDonald, Gordon. *A Resilient Life*. Nashville: Nelson, 2004.

Malphurs, Aubrey. *Maximizing Your Effectiveness: How to Discover and Develop Your Divine Design*. Grand Rapids MI: Baker, 1995.

McNeal, Reggie. *A Work of Heart*. San Francisco: Jossey-Bass, 2000.

Morrell, Margot, and Stephanie Capparell. *Shackleton's Way: Leadership Lessons from the Great Antarctic Explorer*. New York: Penguin, 2001.

Mulholland, M. Robert. *Invitation to a Journey*. Downers Grove, IL: InterVarsity, 1993.

Ogden, Greg. *Discipleship Essentials: A Guide to Building Your Life in Christ*. Downers Grove, IL: InterVarsity, 1998.

Ogden, Greg, and Daniel Meyer. *Leadership Essentials*. Downers Grove, IL: InterVarsity, 2007.

Packer, J. I. *A Passion for Faithfulness*. Wheaton, IL: Crossway, 1995.

Patterson, Jerry L., and Paul Kelleher. *Resilient School Leaders*. Alexandria, VA: Association for Supervision and Curriculum Development, 2005.

Reeves, Rodney. *Spirituality According to Paul*. Downers Grove, IL: IVP Academic, 2011.

Scazzero, Peter. *The Emotionally Healthy Church*. Grand Rapids, MI: Zondervan, 2003.

———. *Emotionally Healthy Spirituality*. Nashville: Nelson, 2006.

Seamands, Stephen. *Ministry in the Image of God*. Downers Grove, IL: InterVarsity, 2005.

Searby, Mark. "The Ministry of Mentoring" (unpublished manuscript, January 24, 2012), Microsoft Word file.

Siebert, Al. *The Five Levels of Resiliency*. Portland, OR: Al Siebert Resiliency Center, n.d. http://resiliencycenter.com/the-five-levels-of-resiliency/

Sisk, Ronald D. *The Competent Pastor*. Herndon, VA: The Alban Institute, 2005.

Stanley, Paul, and J. Robert Clinton. *Connecting: The Mentoring Relationships You Need to Succeed in Life*. Colorado Springs, CO: NavPress, 1992.

Stott, John R. W. *Basic Christian Leadership*. Downers Grove, IL: InterVarsity, 2002.

———. *God's New Society*. Downers Grove, IL: InterVarsity, 1979.

Thielman, Frank. *Theology of the New Testament*. Grand Rapids, MI: Zondervan, 2005.

Thompson, Marjorie J. *Soul Feast*. Louisville, KY: Westminster John Knox, 2005.

Tidball, Derek. *Ministry by the Book*. Downers Grove, IL: InterVarsity, 2008.

———. *Skillful Shepherds*. Grand Rapids, MI: Zondervan, 1986.

Tripp, Paul David. *Dangerous Calling*. Wheaton, IL: Crossway Books, 2012.

Webster, Douglas D. *Living in Tension: A Theology of Ministry, Vol. Two*. Eugene, OR: Cascade, 2012.

Westberg, Granger. *Good Grief: 50th Anniversary Edition*. Philadelphia: Fortress, 2011.

Willard, Dallas. "Spiritual Formation in Christ: A Perspective on What It Is and How It Might Be Done." In Todd W. Hall and Mark R. McMinn, eds. *Spiritual Formation, Counseling, and Psychotherapy*, 3–9. Hauppauge, NY: Nova Science, 2003.

Williams, Brian A. *The Potter's Rib: Mentoring for Pastoral Formation*. Vancouver: Regent College Publishing, 2005.

Willimon, William H. *Pastor: The Theology and Practice of Ordained Ministry*. Nashville: Abingdon, 2002.

Witt, Lance. *Replenish*. Grand Rapids, MI: Baker, 2011.

Zachary, Lois J. *The Mentee's Guide*. San Francisco: Jossey-Bass, 2009.

———. *The Mentor's Guide*. San Francisco: Jossey-Bass, 2000.

CONTRIBUTORS

Lyle Dorsett is the Billy Graham Professor of Evangelism at Beeson Divinity School, Samford University, in Birmingham, Alabama and also serves as the Rector of Christ the King Anglican Church in Birmingham. He holds the PhD from the University of Missouri. Lyle has published more than twenty books, including *Seeking the Secret Place: The Spiritual Formation of C. S. Lewis.*

Rick Grace is the senior pastor of Spring Creek Fellowship in Springdale, Arkansas. Rick has served as a pastor for more than thirty years. He holds the DMin from Dubuque Seminary in Dubuque, Iowa where he studied with Donald Bloesch. Rick also teaches as an adjunct professor at John Brown University, Ecclesia College, and at Beeson Divinity School.

Randy Hemphill is founder and director of LIFE Ministries in Chelsea, Alabama. He and his wife, Melody, conduct numerous marriage seminars each year and are involved in one-on-one mentoring with pastoral couples. Randy has his DMin from Beeson Divinity School.

Jason McConnell is senior pastor of Franklin United Church in Franklin, Vermont. He has served there for twelve years. Jason has the MDiv and MTh from Gordon-Conwell Seminary and is a 2012 graduate of Beeson Divinity School with a DMin degree. He also leads seminars for the RHMA.

Contributors

Tim McCoy is senior pastor of Ingleside Baptist Church in Macon, Georgia. He has served there for twenty-five years. He is a graduate of the Southern Baptist Theological Seminary with a PhD in New Testament. He also teaches as an adjunct professor for Beeson Divinity School.

Todd Parmenter is the Administrative Pastor of Northwoods Community Church in Peoria, Illinois. He has served as an administrator for churches for fifteen years. He is a graduate of Trinity International University with a BA in Business and is a trained facilitator for Financial Peace University.

Chuck Sackett is senior minister of the Madison Park Christian Church in Quincy, Illinois. Chuck has the DMin degree from Trinity Evangelical Divinity School. He is a professor of homiletics for Lincoln Christian Seminary in Lincoln, Illinois. Chuck travels worldwide teaching preaching and leadership seminars.

Shawn Shannon is Director of Baptist Student Ministries at Mary Hardin- Baylor University in Texas. She recently completed her fourteenth year there. She is a 2008 graduate of Beeson Divinity School with the DMin degree.

Dick Wamsley is a retired pastor of the Christian Churches/ Churches of Christ. Dick recently left a twenty-four-year pastorate at the Taylorville Christian Church in Taylorville, Illinois. He holds the MDiv from Lincoln Christian Seminary and has studied at the doctoral level at TEDS. Dick also served as president of Nebraska Christian College from 1984–1990 after serving there eight years as Dean of Students.

Chris Winford is the senior pastor at the First Baptist Church in Brunswick, Georgia. Chris began his ministry there in 2014. He is a 2011 graduate of Beeson Divinity School with the DMin degree.